Risk Regulation Lessons from Mad Cows

Risk Regulation Lessons from Mad Cows

Joseph E. Aldy

Harvard University
Cambridge, MA 02138
USA
joseph_aldy@hks.harvard.edu

W. Kip Viscusi

Vanderbilt University Law School
Nashville, TN 37203
USA
kip.viscusi@vanderbilt.edu

now
the essence of knowledge

Boston – Delft

Foundations and Trends® in Microeconomics

Published, sold and distributed by:
now Publishers Inc.
PO Box 1024
Hanover, MA 02339
USA
Tel. +1-781-985-4510
www.nowpublishers.com
sales@nowpublishers.com

Outside North America:
now Publishers Inc.
PO Box 179
2600 AD Delft
The Netherlands
Tel. +31-6-51115274

The preferred citation for this publication is J. E. Aldy and W. K. Viscusi, Risk Regulation Lessons from Mad Cows, Foundation and Trends® in Microeconomics, vol 8, no 4, pp 231–313, 2012

ISBN: 978-1-60198-764-8

Editorial Scope

Foundations and Trends® in Microeconomics will publish survey and tutorial articles in the following topics:

- Environmental Economics
  - Contingent Valuation
  - Environmental Health Risks
  - Climate Change
  - Endangered Species
  - Market-based Policy Instruments
- Health Economics
  - Moral Hazard
  - Medical Care Markets
  - Medical Malpractice
  - Insurance economics
- Industrial Organization
  - Theory of the Firm
  - Regulatory Economics
  - Market Structure
  - Auctions
  - Monopolies and Antitrust
  - Transaction Cost Economics
- Labor Economics
  - Labor Supply
  - Labor Demand
  - Labor Market Institutions
  - Search Theory
  - Wage Structure
  - Income Distribution
  - Race and Gender
- Law and Economics
  - Models of Litigation
  - Crime
  - Torts, Contracts and Property
  - Constitutional Law
- Public Economics
  - Public Goods
  - Environmental Taxation
  - Social Insurance
  - Public Finance
  - International Taxation

Information for Librarians

Foundations and Trends® in Microeconomics, 2012, Volume 8, 4 issues. ISSN paper version 1547-9846. ISSN online version 1547-9854. Also available as a combined paper and online subscription.

Foundations and Trends® in
Microeconomics
Vol. 8, No. 4 (2012) 231–313

DOI: 10.1561/0700000046

Risk Regulation Lessons from Mad Cows*

Joseph E. Aldy[1] and W. Kip Viscusi[2]

[1] *John F. Kennedy School of Government, Harvard University, 79 JFK Street, Cambridge, MA 02138, USA, joseph_aldy@hks.harvard.edu*
[2] *Vanderbilt University Law School, 131 21st Avenue South, Nashville, TN 37203, kip.viscusi@vanderbilt.edu*

Abstract

The mad cow disease crisis in the United Kingdom (U.K.) was a major policy disaster. The government and public health officials failed to identify the risk to humans, created tremendous uncertainty regarding the human risks once they were identified, and undertook a series of policies that undermined public trust. In contrast, the mad cow disease risk never became a major problem in the United States (U.S.). The lead time that the U.S. had in responding to the disease that was first identified in the U.K. assisted in planning the policy response to avert a crisis. The absence of a comparable U.S. crisis, however, does not imply that the U.S. risk management approach was a success. Until recently, there was no systematic assessment of the domestic risks of mad cow disease. Moreover, U.S. government agencies have never undertaken a

*This research was supported by a cooperative agreement with the USDA Economic Research Service. The authors bear sole responsibility for the contents and policy views expressed. Eleanor McCormick provided outstanding research assistance. Laurel Donahue superbly handled reference checking and all phases of manuscript production. The authors thank Marsha Cohen, David Just, Tom Kniesner, and participants of the 2007 ERS PREISM workshop for valuable comments on an earlier draft.

comprehensive assessment of the benefits and costs of any U.S. regulation dealing with mad cow disease. The absence of a sound economic basis for policy is reflected in the United States Department of Agriculture's (USDA) ill-considered decision to prohibit the private testing of beef for mad cow disease. This decision disadvantaged companies that sought such testing in order to comply with foreign testing regulations. In the absence of such testing, U.S. beef exports plummeted. One company that attempted to implement a testing program launched a legal challenge to the USDA prohibition and was unsuccessful. The policy failures in both the U.K. and the U.S. provide several lessons for regulating invasive species risks and dealing with emerging risks more generally. We conclude with a series of ten public policy lessons for dealing with similar emerging risks.

Contents

1

Introduction

The mad cow disease outbreak in the United Kingdom (U.K.) and the emergence of the new variant Creutzfeldt–Jakob disease (vCJD) in humans is one of the most prominent international risk crises of the past two decades. Beginning in the early 1990s, the U.K. had annual totals of thousands of cattle affected by bovine spongiform encephalopathy (BSE). There were fears that people would also be exposed to related disease risks. Once the link to humans was identified, some scientists estimated that the toll among people would be of a similar catastrophic magnitude. Although the mass carnage that many predicted did not occur, the U.K. mad cow experience is widely regarded as a major policy debacle. Scientists and government officials were slow to identify and acknowledge the mad cow risks to humans. Once the dangers became apparent, the risk estimates that were generated spanned enormous ranges and proved to be wildly inaccurate. Government officials lost credibility with the public, which viewed the government as being captured by agricultural industry interests.

In contrast, one might view the United States (U.S.) experience as an unqualified success. The crisis that emerged in the U.K. did not take hold in the U.S. Very few U.S. cattle have had the disease, and there are no documented human cases attributable to BSE exposures originating in the United States. The February 2008 announcement of the largest beef recall in U.S. history resulting from a meat-packing company failing to comply with United States Department of Agriculture (USDA) inspection rules motivated by BSE risks raises questions about the U.S. risk management system (Schafer, 2008; Pacelle, 2008).

As we will show in this article, the absence of a comparable crisis in the U.S. does not signal that the mad cow experience has been a U.S. policy success story. The exposure to potential BSE risks is quite different in the U.S. so that the dangers were not great. Given the policy lead time afforded by the crisis emerging first in the U.K., U.S. policyholders had an opportunity to design and evaluate reasoned policy responses to the potential hazards. Yet there was little attempt to formulate a meaningful risk assessment and, to date, there has yet to be a full blown assessment of the benefits and costs of any regulatory initiative related to BSE or vCJD.

The main policy failures have been substantive as well. In situations of potential product risks, one might expect the government to encourage firms to test the safety of their products. In this instance, however, the government took the opposite position, prohibiting private testing of beef for the presence of BSE. This restrictive policy in turn led an affected company to fight the testing ban in *Creekstone Farms Premium Beef, L.L.C. v. U.S. Dept. of Agriculture et al.*[1] As we will show below, the testing prohibition not only blocks testing efforts that have a sound economic basis but also fails to account for the realities of the international regulatory environment.

Based on the mad cow experience, it is also possible to draw a number of lessons regarding how one should regulate invasive species risks and deal with dimly understood but potentially serious risks to large populations. BSE and vCJD have several commonalities with other types of risks and with other risks addressed by invasive species management policies. The risks are novel and uncertain, which is often the case with newly emerging hazards. The latency period before the

[1] *Creekstone Farms Premium Beef, L.L.C. v. U.S. Dept. of Agriculture et al.*, 517 F. Supp.2d 8 (D.D.C. Mar. 29, 2007).

disease becomes manifested is uncertain and complicates the problem of forming accurate risk assessments. In addition, often policymakers had to take actions such as the 1997 U.S. feed ban not only before the risk levels were well understood but also before the basic scientific linkages were fully established.

The issues raised by the mad cow crisis also have important international dimensions. The BSE outbreak in the U.K. raised questions about the safety of beef exports from the U.K. and also led other countries to restrict imports from the U.K. Similarly, the identification in the U.S. of a cow from Canada which had BSE led to concerns about the importation of cattle elsewhere. In response to the uncertainty about the level of the risk and other countries' restrictions on imports, at least one beef producer made a concerted effort to have its beef tested for BSE, which then led to action by the USDA to suppress this initiative.

Examination of the mad cow experience provides an instructive vantage point for assessing the soundness of the policy response to this type of risk and to develop guidelines for how government policies might respond to future crises.[2] Although the substantive focus of our analysis will be on mad cow disease and invasive species risks, many of the characteristics of the risk problem are shared by other hazards. For example, the hazards posed by terrorism and nanotechnology raise similar classes of concerns. In the case of terrorism, the risks are quite uncertain, not well understood even by experts in the field, but may nevertheless pose a real threat to large numbers of people. Nanotechnology likewise has similar characteristics, with the added complication that whatever risks are posed by nanotechnology may not be evident for many years, long after millions have been exposed to nano particles and whatever associated risks of illness there might be.

Our exploration of the mad cow crisis begins in Section 2 with an examination of the nature of risks to animals and humans from BSE and vCJD. Knowing what the disease is represents a useful starting point, but the size of the exposed population and the likelihood of being infected by the disease are also relevant, as these will determine the

[2] Ian Sample (2007) observes that some are predicting that "two future waves of vCJD could strike in the next 10 to 50 years."

overall consequences of the hazard. We motivate and present a mainstream public policy framework to evaluate the welfare consequences of BSE and vCJD risk mitigation instruments in Section 3. A key component of this policy evaluation is the question of how one should assess these risks. The ways in which others have conceptualized the risks for policy purposes are examined in Section 4. How the government should communicate newly emerging risks remains a daunting task. Should the government adopt a precautionary approach and focus on upper bounds to be "better safe than sorry" or should risk assessments be more balanced? After providing a chronology of the policy events and policy actions in Section 5, we examine issues pertaining to media coverage and risk communication in Section 6, consumer responses to the informational environment in Section 7, and governments' use of trade policy in Section 8. The controversial effort by one beef producer to have its beef certified as being BSE-free brings together a wide set of cross-cutting issues of risk communication, government regulation, litigation, and international trade, and will serve as the main policy case study in Section 9. In Section 10, we summarize general lessons for regulatory policy derived from this experience.

2

Background on BSE and vCJD

A useful starting point is to explore the source of BSE risks to cattle and the relation of mad cow disease to vCJD risks to humans. The risks of mad cow for cattle and humans rank among the most serious and most highly publicized risks that might affect consumers. In recognition of the threat, media coverage has been considerable and the overall magnitudes of the risks are becoming well known. Indeed, the television coverage of staggering cattle affected with BSE has created a strong visual image of the consequences of BSE in much the same way as the Love Canal coverage enabled the public to visualize the reality of hazardous waste exposures.[1] Given general public knowledge of the main features of BSE and vCJD, here we provide a brief summary by way of background, which we will subsequently refine below.[2]

Although all the scientific issues have not been resolved, the leading causal theory is that BSE is caused by an abnormally configured

[1] The largest beef recall in U.S. history announced in February 2008 by the Westland/Hallmark Meat Company provided another opportunity for national news coverage to show video of downer cows when noting the potential risk that such cows have BSE (Risling, 2008; Martin, 2008).

[2] See Lister and Becker (2007) and van Zwanenberg and Millstone (2005) for further background summaries.

protein, the prion protein PrP (proteinaceous infectious particle). Thus, these prions cause otherwise normal proteins to become abnormal. The origin of the protein has been traced to a scrapie agent in sheep and in rendered protein that overcame the species barrier. Thus, the first somewhat surprising aspect of the disease is that it is thought to have spread from sheep to cows. The mechanism of transmittal is through the food chain. That BSE emerged as a major problem in the 1990s and not earlier appears to be likely due to the change in the feeding system in the 1970s. The introduction of meat and bone meal as a protein supplement in feed for cows creates the potential for transmittal of BSE if the original animal had BSE. Unfortunately, there is no evidence of any immune response to the agent that might otherwise serve a protective function. Exposure to the prion protein PrP has dire consequences for the animal.

BSE has uniformly adverse consequences for the infected cattle. There is first a long incubation period of 3 to 5 years for the infected cattle. The length of the incubation period also may affect the extent of infectivity as the elapsed time since the infection and the age of the animal are key determinants of the risk (Cohen et al. 2001). Thus, cattle may have contracted BSE but no physical or pre-mortem testable disease indications are apparent. After the incubation period, the disease becomes slowly progressive, leading to deterioration of the animal's brain, which in turn disrupts a wide range of cognitive functions. The disease is always fatal to the infected animal.

The disease profile of vCJD for humans is in many respects quite similar. An incubation period is followed by a slowly progressive deterioration in brain functions and ultimately the individual's death. The food chain, in this case eating infected beef or other infected meat, is the mechanism of exposure. That the disease could be transmitted from sheep to cows was somewhat surprising. Even more surprising from a scientific standpoint was the crossing of the species barrier from animals to humans. The disease vCJD is distinguished from its genetic counterpart, CJD, by the mechanism of exposure. Thus, the human risk from BSE is vCJD, while CJD predates this new form of illness and will not be affected by BSE policies.

Thus far, vCJD has posed a fairly small probability of illness for humans, with about 200 fatalities worldwide through early 2013, as compared to the much larger risk that BSE poses to animals, where tens of thousands have died from BSE and many more have been killed to prevent the spread of the disease. For both BSE and vCJD, the risk outcomes are fatal and involve very high morbidity costs as well. These risks also are not well understood, particularly for humans, so that there is considerable imprecision in our knowledge of the hazards. We have, however, moved from a situation of complete ignorance of the human risk to a situation of substantial uncertainty regarding the risk probabilities, and it is likely that the magnitude of the risk will continue to be understood more precisely.

3

Public Policy Framework

These characteristics of BSE and vCJD highlight the existence of market failures that provide a potential rationale for government regulation of these risks. That there might be a potential governmental role does not necessarily imply that all kinds of government intervention will be beneficial. As we discuss below, the U.S. government's attempt to prohibit companies from certifying the safety of their product appears to be particularly unresponsive to the kinds of market failures that provide the impetus for a governmental role. Similarly, the official efforts in the U.K. to dismiss the risk and its importance likewise fell short of any reasonable welfare-enhancing norm.

First, novel and potentially unexpected risks may motivate either an inadequate or excessive response, each socially sub-optimal, by consumers and producers. Consider the effect of risk ignorance on the part of consumers and producers as well as the other extreme case of exaggerated perceptions of the risk. Uninformed consumers take no efforts to acquire information or mitigate their exposure to a novel and likely unknown-to-many risk. Uninformed producers likewise take no reputation-protecting or liability-minimizing actions to reduce the supply of a novel or unknown risk. Alternatively, consumers and producers could overestimate the risk — either its magnitude or its probability — and their reactions could impose significant welfare losses (see our discussion below on risk ambiguity and Aldy and Viscusi, 2013). As a result, surveillance for novel risks could provide socially valuable public information about the presence and level of risks. The design of surveillance to provide this public good can be informed by experiences addressing novel risks in other countries. Indeed, in the case of invasive species risks such as BSE, surveillance at the point of entry in the supply chain could benefit from the efficacy of practices addressing this risk in other countries.

Second, consumers lack information about the potential for BSE contamination in specific beef products. There is no potential for information acquisition based on consumer actions, which in turn has ramifications for producers. A consumer cannot identify a BSE-infected product at the grocery or restaurant. There is no immediate sign, such as odor or discoloration, that serves as a marker for BSE. Moreover, the latency in developing symptoms of vCJD further complicates identification of a specific consumption event that led to contracting the disease. As a result, firms cannot easily build a reputation for quality, BSE-free repeatedly consumed "experience" products. The only potentially effective avenue for information provision derives from some kind of certification effort rather than consumer observations and experiences with the product.

This information asymmetry also applies to the long list of intermediaries in the supply chain for beef. A restaurant may not know if the sourced beef was processed in a slaughterhouse with BSE-infected cows. A slaughterhouse may not know if the sourced cattle were exposed to BSE-infected feed. So the information asymmetry closely resembles symmetric incomplete information for which it becomes very difficult for consumers to discern high-quality ("low" BSE risk) from low-quality ("high" BSE risk) beef, and limited private means are available for producers to remedy this information problem (Antle, 2001). Indeed, it raises questions on how regulators can design instruments to address incomplete information (an issue we return to later in this section and in Section 9 on testing).

Third, habit formation could motivate a paternalistic justification for government regulation. Habitual behavior can emerge even within the context of fully rational, optimizing consumers. A consumer who has a long history of eating beef products with no apparent ill effects will have formed relatively precise risk beliefs based on these experiences. Given such a strong information base, consumers will have relatively precise probabilistic beliefs that will tend to limit the degree to which beliefs are updated with new information. Learning about the risk level is both limited and, in the case of direct consumer experiences, not feasible. If consumers become infected, the irreversible nature of the health effects will impede any attempts to limit one's risk through adaptive behavioral responses. Even with good information, an individual may not reduce beef consumption to mitigate BSE risk due to self-control problems. This decision imposes costs on the future version of this individual, what some have termed an "internality" in the context of diet and smoking, and thus the failure for the individual to reduce consumption now would result in regret by that individual in the future.

Fourth, erroneous consumption decisions are consequential because the stakes are high. The health risks involved entail irreversible health effects in which there is both a fatality risk as well as accompanying morbidity consequences. Small probability-severe consequence events pose both challenges for individual decision-making and frequently provide the impetus for government regulation, especially when there are severe barriers to informed individual choice as there are in this instance.

Fifth, the role of international trade may provide another rationale for a government regulator to intervene in the market to mitigate BSE risk. Suppose that country A's domestic beef market is supplied by domestic production and imports from country B. If country B reports a case of a BSE-infected cow, then country A's only instrument to assure its domestic consumers that the retail beef supply is safe from BSE is to ban imports from country B. Otherwise, the information problems consumers face in the market — and their inability to identify BSE-free from potentially BSE-infected beef, or even to discern foreign versus domestic sourced beef — could result in a significant unraveling of the market and drop in consumption. Thus, producers in country A would push for a trade ban to assure quality in the domestic market, and hence continued demand for their product. As a result, producers in country B may also have an incentive to request regulatory interventions by the government in country B to reduce the probability of a BSE infection in order to keep open their export markets.

While identifying market failures is necessary to justify a public policy intervention on welfare grounds, it is not sufficient. Poorly designed regulations could impose societal costs greater than societal benefits and thus result in a government failure that exacerbates the welfare loss associated with the market failure. Even a regulation that delivers benefits greater than costs may not be the most cost-effective or efficient way to tackle the problem. A formal framework that requires the quantification and monetization of benefits and costs of various policy options to mitigate BSE risk can serve to identify those that maximize net social welfare. Such analysis informs the design of cost-effective instruments and could also identify combinations of instruments that could be most efficacious and welfare-enhancing.

To evaluate the benefits of potential government interventions to mitigate BSE risk, the regulator needs to identify various categories of benefits. For example, reducing BSE risk can reduce cattle illness and mortality and reduce human mortality via transmission and development of vCJD. These health benefits include both morbidity and mortality effects. In addition, the anxiety produced by fears of BSE risks can potentially be alleviated through government regulation that ensures a low level of risk. Given consumer and foreign government responses to BSE cases, reducing BSE risk can also deliver benefits to producers by ensuring their reputation for high-quality ("low" BSE risk) beef and hence demand for their products. Then, the regulator needs to determine the efficacy of various policy instruments in delivering positive outcomes in each of these benefit categories. For example, a ban on ruminant protein in cattle feed can reduce BSE transmission risk to other cattle and to humans, while a ban on blood donations from individuals who lived in the U.K. during the 1990s is intended only to address human mortality risk. Once the relevant benefit categories have been identified for a given policy intervention, then the regulator must undertake a quantitative risk assessment of the baseline risk associated with BSE and the change in risk associated with the policy instrument. Given the importance of risk assessment in the context of BSE and vCJD, we focus in significant detail on this issue in the following section. The change in the likelihood of an adverse BSE or vCJD event can then be monetized, say by the value of a typical head of cattle for bovine mortality, the value of statistical life for human mortality, and by the decline in profits for producers if consumers buy less of their product or foreign markets ban their goods.

To evaluate the costs of a policy intervention, the regulator must estimate the direct costs of any requirements under a new rule as well as how firms may respond to the regulation. For example, a tracking and traceability system for cattle and beef can play an important role in a BSE surveillance program but also imposes costs on cattle producers, processors, marketers, and retailers. Throughout the supply chain, firms need to maintain the records and undertake relevant expenses associated with tracking their cattle and beef throughput. The elasticities of consumer demand, domestic supply, and foreign supply will determine the economic incidence of such interventions. The aggregate foregone surplus of consumers and suppliers determines the cost of the intervention.

In estimating the benefits and costs of a policy intervention, it is important to recognize and account for the endogeneity of consumer and producer behavior. For example, an information intervention (such as labeling premised on a surveillance system) is effective only if consumers adjust their behavior in response to this information. Indeed, risk assessments that fail to account for avoidance behavior may yield inaccurate measures of risk and incomplete estimates of the welfare costs posed by BSE risk (and hence the benefits available for interventions that mitigate such risk). Producers may also respond to various government interventions. For example, we describe in detail the case of a U.S. producer that used BSE testing of its beef in an effort to regain access to lucrative foreign markets such as Japan in Section 9.

The empirical challenge for novel risks like BSE and vCJD lies in estimating the efficacy of various policy options. By definition, there may be little experience in combating novel risks, although there are potential opportunities to learn from interventions undertaken by other countries that initially faced such risks. There may be few natural experiments from which to estimate efficacy. As a result, risk assessment of policy interventions may require some strong assumptions and the robustness of the preferred policy options to the choice of assumptions should be carefully examined. We explore this issue in the case of BSE and vCJD in the next two sections.

In light of the information problem characterizing BSE and vCJD, it is perhaps unsurprising that regulators have frequently adopted the rather blunt policy instrument of a ban to reduce BSE risk. For example, regulators have banned imports of cattle and/or beef from countries that report cases of BSE-infected cows. Regulators implemented a feed ban that prohibited the use of (potentially BSE-infected) ruminant protein. U.S. regulators also banned blood donations from individuals who lived in the U.K. or certain European countries for specified periods of time. We address the efficacy and efficiency of these policy instruments in further detail in our discussion of risk assessment in the next section.

4

Risk Analysis Principles

As we note above, the general economic maxim for efficient policies is that they should be designed to maximize the spread between expected policy benefits and costs. While this efficiency guideline may appear to be innocuous, very few U.S. risk regulations policies adhere to this approach.[1] Typically, the agency's legislative mandate imposes a more risk-oriented approach that does not permit proper balancing of competing risk concerns. Indeed, the Clean Air Act prohibits the consideration of costs in the setting of national ambient air quality standards. One notable exception to the failure to balance benefits and costs is the U.S. Department of Transportation, for which there is strong adherence to promulgating policies for which the benefits exceed the costs. In the absence of any restrictive legislative mandates that would prohibit the USDA from undertaking benefit-cost balancing for regulations pertaining to invasive species risks, we assume that the U.S. and presumably other countries as well have the freedom to design policies that can address risks of BSE and vCJD in a balanced manner.

[1] Refer to Aldy and Viscusi (2013) for further elaboration of the U.S. experience with risk regulations.

Irrespective of whether the policy can reflect a true balancing of benefit and cost concerns, the focus should be on the "expected" risk reduction benefits. Focusing on the "expected" consequences of a policy has specific consequences for how the risk assessment should enter the analysis. Thus, what should guide decisions is the mean value of the risk probability. For vCJD risks, what is the average probability of contracting the disease across the population? Other formulations of risk assessments are possible and, indeed, are frequently adopted by U.S. government agencies. Rather than asking what is the average expected value of the risk or what is the best estimate of the level of the risk, agencies focus on "conservative" estimates of the risk. Worst case scenarios rather than reasonable expectations are the guide. By definition, these conservative risk assessments will overstate the actual level of the risk because they pertain to the risk value at the upper tail of the risk distribution, such as the 95th percentile, or in the case of the EPA, hazardous waste assessments, a risk value beyond the 99th percentile (Hamilton and Viscusi, 1999).

How much such conservative risk assessments distort the actual mean level of the risk depends on the structure of the risk analysis calculation and the degree of conservatism in each component of the calculation. Suppose for concreteness that policymakers focus on the 95th percentile of the distribution for each of the parameters used in forming the risk assessment parameters rather than simply using values based on some more vaguely defined worst case scenario. If this is done for only a single component, such as the ultimate vCJD risk, then there will be a 0.05 chance that the expected risk level is as great as is being estimated. This kind of single conservatism assumption, however, greatly understates the extent of conservatism biases that might be engendered and typically are engendered through the risk conservatism approach. Suppose that the calculation involves 3 parameters — the vCJD risk posed by the meat supply, the quantity of beef eaten by the person, and the probability that eating the infected beef will lead to vCJD. If these parameters are independently distributed and each of these parameters is set at the 95th percentile of their distribution, then the chance that the risk will be as great as is estimated will only be $0.05 \times 0.05 \times 0.05$, which is less than 2 in 10,000.

The main difficulty with the conservatism approach is that if one adopts this conservative methodology it distorts the information available for policy making. Often the actual expected risk is not known, as policymakers may see only the endpoint conservative risk estimate. Focusing on worst case scenarios poses particular dangers with respect to mad cow risks and the counterpart vCJD risks. The hazards posed by these risks are very imprecisely understood. Excessive attention to the worst case scenario will lead to a targeting of policy resources on risks that have very little chance of being as great as is actually assumed, thus diverting attention from real threats and imposing needless costs. Such an approach disproportionately diverts funds to complicated, poorly understood risks and away from simpler, better understood risks. Poorly understood risks would have a larger spread in their distributions, so the 95th percentile of a poorly understood risk is likely to be much more different from its mean than the 95th percentile for a well-understood risk. Complicated risks — those with many uncertain components — would then magnify this divergence between "worst case" risk and expected risk to a much greater degree than simpler risks with fewer uncertain components. The extent to which there have been enormous gaps in our knowledge of these risks will be apparent upon reviewing the U.K. risk analysis experience.

In addition to undertaking a sound risk analysis grounded in the principles for efficient policy design, policymakers should incorporate risk analysis in their policy decisions. In the U.K., where the mad cow issues were first confronted in a serious way, some observers suggested that the government response appeared to be driven more by political pressures than by a reasoned response to risk.[2] Skepticism of the government's trustworthiness is also reflected in public opinion polls, as the U.K. public believed that the government was more concerned with protecting farmers than the general public.[3] Indeed, the government in the U.K. fostered an environment of uncertainty even after the risk had

[2] This is a major theme of van Zwanenberg and Millstone (2005).

[3] The April 1996 Gallup England poll reported the following results with respect to the question "which group do you think the government is concerned to protect more, farmers or the general public?:" farmers: 46 percent; general public: 21 percent; both: 12 percent; neither: 15 percent; and don't know: 5 percent.

become apparent. In the early period of the BSE outbreak, there was the expected resistance to regulation from the cattle industry. There have been allegations that the same kinds of political pressures conceivably may have been at work in the U.S. Critics of the U.S. Department of Agriculture have charged that the agency had been captured by the cattle industry. Dale Moore, the chief of staff of the Secretary of Agriculture, had been the chief lobbyist for the National Cattlemen's Beef Association (Schlosser, 2004). The Agency's spokeswoman, Alisa Harrison, issued press releases for the USDA with titles such as "Mad Cow Disease Not a Problem in the U.S." (Schlosser, 2004). She formerly had served as the director of public relations for the National Cattlemen's Beef Association. If the hazards had become apparent and more highly publicized, the locus of the strongest political pressures in all likelihood would have shifted to consumers and the general public. While financial interests presumably were paramount for beef producers, a concern with product health risks was the dominant public concern.

How the public will react to such risks depends not only on the expected risk level but also on other dimensions of the risk. One such dimension is the extent of risk ambiguity. The risk judgments the public will form in such instances will be highly imprecise. Risk information provided to them will also be imprecise and may foster the perception of ambiguity by indicating a possibly substantial risk range. In the presence of such ambiguity, for low risks such as vCJD people will exhibit ambiguity aversion. Thus, for example, if there is 50–50 chance that the risk could take on a low value p_1 or a high value p_2, then people will tend to treat the risk as being greater than the average of the two risks. This risk ambiguity aversion is a well documented form of individual irrationality (Ellsberg, 1961; Fox and Tversky, 1995; Viscusi and Chesson, 1999).

A particularly striking case of risk ambiguity aversion occurs when there are risk experts with opposing points of view.[4] Conflicting risk assessments from a single institution generate a modest ambiguity aversion effect. However, the impact of risk ambiguity is much more pronounced if the experts are from different institutions. For example,

[4] See Viscusi (1997) for the basis of this analysis of the effect of such a risk debate.

if there is disagreement between a government risk expert and a meat industry risk expert, people will tend to dismiss the low risk assessment and gravitate toward the worst case scenario as their risk belief.

The result is that there will be substantial public pressures to over-regulate imprecisely understood risks, such as those posed by BSE and vCJD. For other countries considering imports of beef for which there is some uncertain potential risk, there will also be inordinate pressures to exclude such imports, creating support for rigid protectionist policies.

The absence of full information about the level of the risk creates opportunities for learning and refining risk beliefs. From the vantage point of the U.S., the cost associated with much of the learning is minimal. The natural experiment taking place in the U.K. provided a considerable information base about assessing the risk to cattle and to people. The U.S. was quite fortunate with respect to the timing in that the evidence on the foreign mad cow "experiments" would be known before the first case was discovered in the U.S., making it possible to formulate more informed policy decisions to reduce risks that later might have affected the U.S. Thus, the U.S. benefited from the first major BSE outbreak occurring elsewhere, giving U.S. regulators an opportunity to assess the risk and formulate a policy response.

Despite these advantages with respect to information acquisition, there are limits as well. The small individual probabilities of vCJD limit the informational content of the evidence regarding the exposure of even a large population. The incubation periods before BSE becomes manifested in cattle introduce one element of delay, and there is an additional lag before the vCJD becomes manifested in people, creating a temporal gap that makes inferences less clear-cut. Unlike the task of sorting out the causes of acute accidents, it is often difficult to trace the exposure that led to vCJD many years later. Because the symptoms of the illness are not unique to vCJD, but are shared for example by CJD, it is not a signature disease for which the nature of the ailment would be well understood. Making a precise prediction of the risks of BSE and vCJD in the U.S. is also complicated by the lack of precise information on the extent of compliance with the U.S. Food and Drug Administration (FDA) feed ban (Cohen et al., 2001). There may be some feeding of prohibited feed that contains ruminant protein either deliberately, because of a random error in selecting the proper feed, or because of a failure to label the feed correctly. These difficulties are not simply conjectures, as policy assessments by the U.S. Government Accountability Office (U.S. GAO) concluded that the U.S. enforcement efforts have fallen short (U.S. GAO, 2002; Fox and Peterson, 2004). These criticisms have been lodged with respect to inspection databases and the failure to do follow-up inspections with firms found to be in noncompliance with labeling requirements.

Even with the almost two decades of observation of a large number of BSE cases and approximately 200 confirmed vCJD deaths, the underlying science is not well understood. Why the illness crossed the species barrier from animals to humans is still not known. Nor is there any firm evidence making it possible to develop estimates of a dose–response relationship between eating BSE-infected meat and developing vCJD.

In terms of the stages of risk analysis, the first stage of understanding the possible routes of exposure is perhaps most well understood. The primary exposure route for vCJD is from eating BSE-infected meat. It is believed that some cuts of meat are more dangerous than others.[5] On July 9, 2004 the FDA proposed rules to strengthen mad cow safeguards. Included in this was a ban on "specified risk materials (SRMs)" defined as: brain, skull, eyes, trigeminal ganglia, spinal cord, vertebral column (excluding the vertebrae of the tail, the transverse processes of the thoracic and lumbar vertebrae, and the wings of the sacrum) and the dorsal root ganglia of cattle more than 30 months of age. SRMs also include the tonsils and the distal ileum of the small intestine of cattle of any age (FSIS, 2004).

Secondary mechanisms of exposure include blood transfusions, improperly sterilized medical instruments, accidental inoculations, and pharmaceutical and cosmetic products derived from bovine tissue. The

[5] As summarized by Cohen et al. (2001) "The existence and quantity of infectivity in specific tissues depends on the age of the animal and the elapsed time since infection... BSE infectivity potentially available for human consumption can come from specific tissues including cattle brain, spinal cord, cuts of meat with spinal cord or DRG, intestine, and from edible meat contaminated with infectious tissues..." (Section 3.1.4). Appendix Table A.1 summarizes the relative infectivity based on the types of tissue involved.

science becomes even murkier with respect to secondary exposure cases, such as the risk of contracting vCJD from a blood transfusion.

The blood transfusion vCJD risk received substantial recent policy attention to ensure that blood transfusions do not give rise to the next wave of vCJD cases. How great the blood transfusion risks are is not known with any precision. In his 1999 Presidential address to the Royal Statistical Society, Robert N. Curnow outlined many of the problems confronting those attempting to estimate blood transfusion risks for BSE and vCJD. The risks of vCJD from blood transfusions cannot be predicted accurately because of our lack of understanding of many of the fundamental building blocks of any risk analysis.[6] In the U.S., the FDA monitors the safety of the blood supply with respect to BSE risks and has suggested that blood not be accepted from donors who traveled to the U.K. for 3 months or more or lived in Europe for at least 5 years since the BSE outbreak in the U.K. (U.S. GAO, 2002; Gray et al., 2011).[7] Other countries have adopted similar policies, including Canada, Japan, Germany, Australia, New Zealand, and Switzerland (Brown et al., 2001).

Recognizing the blood transfusion risks of vCJD, the U.K. instituted a blood filtering system called leukoreduction beginning in 1999 (Cleemput et al., 2006). This costly procedure was to be used by blood banks in all cases. The costs of U.K. plasma and leucodepletion are quite substantial, on the order of £80 million per year for leucodepletion and an addition £12 million annually for outsourcing plasma (Curnow, 1999). Other precautions with respect to secondary transmission of vCJD include the institution of procedures for the sterilization of medical instruments and recommendations for the usage of disposable instruments (Curnow, 1999).

---

[6] Among the uncertainties that Curnow (1999) identifies are the following: "How much beef and which tissues were consumed at different times and by people of different ages? How infective are the different tissues? Is there a genetic component to human susceptibility to vCJD that will limit the pool of people who can be infected and therefore may be infective?" (p. 466).

[7] According to the FDA, this policy would reduce the pool of donors by about 5 percent, although some estimated potentially significant blood shortages in coastal regions and cities like New York, which imports about one-quarter of its blood supply from Europe. The tightening supply may have caused the 60 percent increase in the prices blood banks charged hospitals over the 1998–2001 period (Gray et al., 2011).

5

Chronology of BSE Events and Policy Actions

Because BSE-infected meat is the causal agent for vCJD, it is instructive to analyze the chronology of events with respect to our knowledge of BSE and to analyze the effect of policy responses on BSE transmission. As indicated in Figure 5.1, the first BSE case was diagnosed in the U.K. in 1986.[1] In 1996 the British government announced a possible link between BSE and vCJD. Through 2012, the U.S. has had a total of four BSE cases. It was not until 2003 that the first case of BSE was found in the U.S. Because the infected cow in the U.S. was of Canadian origin, there was perceived to be a less widespread threat. However, in June 2005, the USDA identified the first indigenous case of BSE found in the U.S. After this Texas cow was found to be BSE-infected, a third cow in Alabama tested as having BSE in March 2006.

The response by the British government to the BSE outbreak led to a dramatic shift in the number of BSE cases reported in the U.K. In 1987 and before there had been a cumulative total of only 446 cases reported (Figure 5.2). However, in 1988 the annual number of recorded BSE cases increased to 2,514, and the number of these cases continued

[1] Appendix Table A.2 summarizes U.K. BSE cases by year, and Appendix Table A.3 presents BSE tallies for other countries.

1985	1990	1995	2000	2005
⇑ **1986** BSE is first diagnosed in the U.K.		⇑ **1996** British government announces possible link between BSE and new variant Creutzfeldt-Jakob Disease (vCJD).	⇑ **2003** USDA announces a single case of BSE. (Cow of Canadian origin).	⇑ **2005** USDA announces the first indigenous case of BSE found in the U.S.

Fig. 5.1 Chronology of events and policy actions.

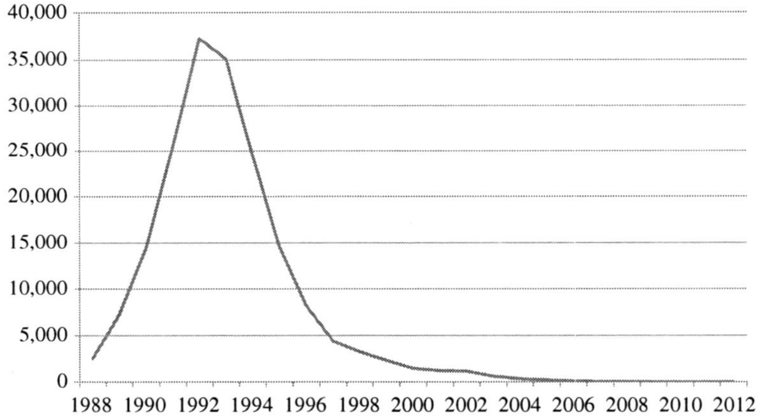

Fig. 5.2 Number of BSE cases reported in the United Kingdom, 1988–2012.

Source: World Organisation for Animal Health, Number of Cases of Bovine Spongiform Encephalopathy (BSE) Reported in the United Kingdom, available at http://www.oie.int/en/animal-health-in-the-world/bse-specific-data/number-of-cases-in-the-united-kingdom/ (last visited November 11, 2013).

to increase until 1992, when the number of reported BSE cases peaked at 37,280. By 2003 the number of reported cases had dropped to under 1,000, then fell to 114 cases in 2006, and only 3 cases were reported in 2012 (World Organisation for Animal Health, 2013b).

While the reduction in the number of BSE cases in the U.K. has been great, the number of annual and total recorded cases still is much greater than in other countries. The U.S. has had only four recorded

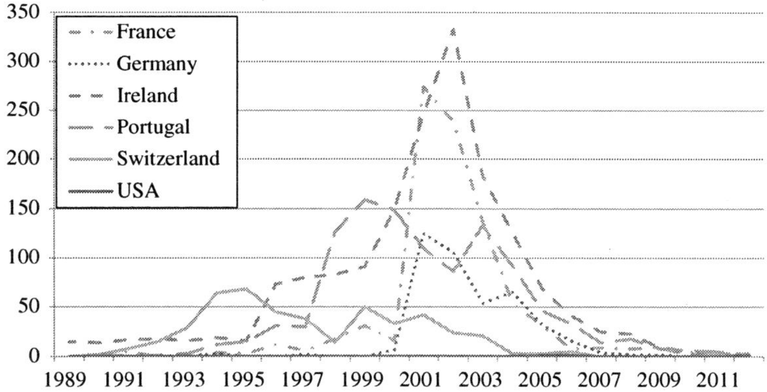

Fig. 5.3 Number of reported BSE cases in farmed cattle worldwide, 1989–2012.

Source: World Organisation for Animal Health, Number of Reported Cases of Bovine Spongiform Encephalopathy (BSE) in Farmed Cattle Worldwide (Excluding the United Kingdom), available at http://www.oie.int/animal-health-in-the-world/bse-specific-data/number-of-reported-cases-worldwide-excluding-the-united-kingdom/, (last visited November 11, 2013).

BSE cases. Moreover, the herd size in the U.S. is much greater than in the U.K. so that the incidence rate is much lower. Some countries have not reported any BSE cases. Other countries, illustrated in Figure 5.3, have not had as favorable an experience as the U.S., but still have had fewer cases than in the U.K.[2] Ireland has had the greatest number of BSE cases other than the U.K., with as many as 333 cases in 2002, although this has declined to only 2 reported cases in 2010. France, Portugal, and to a lesser extent, Germany, have also had significant numbers of BSE cases (World Organisation for Animal Health, 2013c).

As of 2000, no BSE cases had occurred in the U.S. or in any other countries that did not import beef, cattle, or livestock nutritional supplements from the U.K. (Brown et al., 2001; Cherfas, 1990). A prominent hypothesis regarding the emergence of BSE in the U.K. is that the U.K. had a higher proportion of scrapie-infected sheep as well as a higher proportion of these sheep in the mix of rendered animal carcasses. This line of reasoning is consistent with our belief that U.S.

[2] *See* Appendix Table A.3 for supporting data.

policy interventions alone should not receive credit for the relatively unblemished BSE record in the U.S.

What is especially noteworthy about the temporal trajectory of BSE cases in Figure 5.3 is not just the level as compared to the U.K., but also the temporal pattern. Whereas the U.K. BSE cases increased from the late 1980s to a peak in the early 1990s, followed by a steep decline, the main rise in BSE cases outside the U.K. was after that period. Indeed, the most prominent peaks in the prevalence of BSE cases occur after 2000. These countries consequently had the opportunity to observe the British experience with BSE, assess which policies worked and which did not, and also learn that there is in fact a link to humans, making the nature of the threat more pervasive than if restricted to animals alone. This learning from the U.K. experience also had consequences for their willingness to import U.K. beef.

Not surprisingly, the U.K. has also had the greatest number of human fatalities. The annual vCJD death toll in the U.K. is summarized in Table 5.1. These cases include the definite vCJD cases as well as the probable vCJD cases. As of November 2013, there were 177 deaths. The annual death toll peaked at 28 deaths in 2000, 8 years after the peak in BSE cases. If there is a distribution across the population in terms of the extent of the latency period before the illness becomes manifested or heterogeneity in terms of when the illness becomes apparent, then there might continue to be some fatalities observed even after the risk of exposure has been eliminated.

The concentration of the vCJD deaths in the U.K. as compared to the rest of the world is indicated by the data in Table 5.2. This table reports the total number of cases as well as the number who are still alive. The U.K. has by far the greatest number of vCJD cases. The only other country with more than 4 recorded cases is France, which has had 25 cases. Although the U.S. has had 3 documented cases, these individuals all lived for significant periods of time outside the country, where they are believed to have been infected.

The first probable vCJD case in a U.S. resident was that of a Florida woman in her twenties who had grown up in the U.K. According to the CDC, "it is likely that this patient was exposed to the BSE agent one or more times during 1980–1992 before moving to the United States and

Table 5.1. U.K. vCJD Deaths[a].

Referrals of suspect CJD	Deaths of definite and probable CJD
Year	vCJD
1990	—
1991	—
1992	—
1993	—
1994	—
1995	3
1996	10
1997	10
1998	18
1999	15
2000	28
2001	20
2002	17
2003	18
2004	9
2005	5
2006	5
2007	5
2008	2
2009	3
2010	3
2011	5
2012	0
2013	1
Total Referrals	177

[a]As of November 15, 2013, these figures show the number of suspect cases referred to the CJD surveillance unit in Edinburgh and the number of deaths of definite and probable cases in the U.K.
Source: National Creutzfeldt-Jakob Disease Research & Surveillance Unit, University of Edinburgh, CJD Statistics, available at http://www.cjd.ed.ac.uk/documents/figs.pdf (last visited November 13, 2013).

that the interval between the patient's exposure to BSE and onset of illness was 9–21 years. Such an incubation period would be consistent with known incubation periods for other similar diseases in humans, such as kuru and CJD related to exposures to pituitary-derived human growth hormone" (Wiersma et al., 2002) Her death was confirmed in 2004 (Center for Infectious Disease Research and Policy, 2004).

The second reported U.S. case of vCJD was also in a person who had lived in the U.K. from 1980 to 1996 during the period of substantial

Table 5.2. Variant Creutzfeldt-Jakob disease current data through November 2013.

Country	Total number of primary cases (number alive)	Total number of secondary cases: Blood transfusion (number alive)	Cumulative residence in U.K. > 6 months during period 1980–1996
U.K.	174 (0)	3 (0)	177
France	27 (1)	—	1
Republic of Ireland	4 (0)	—	2
Italy	2 (0)	—	0
USA	3[a] (0)	—	2
Canada	2 (0)	—	1
Saudi Arabia	1 (0)	—	0
Japan	1[a] (0)	—	0
Netherlands	3 (0)	—	0
Portugal	2 (0)	—	0
Spain	5 (0)	—	0

[a]The third U.S. patient with vCJD was born and raised in Saudi Arabia and has lived permanently in the United States since late 2005. According to the U.S. case report, the patient was most likely infected as a child when living in Saudi Arabia.
[b]The case from Japan had resided in the U.K. for 24 days in the period 1980–1996.
Source: National Creutzfeldt-Jakob Disease Research & Surveillance Unit, University of Edinburgh, CJD Statistics, *available at* http://www.cjd.ed.ac.uk/documents/worldfigs.pdf (last visited November 15, 2013).

consumer exposure to possibly infected beef.[3] The CDC explicitly ruled out any connection between this case and a BSE-infected cow found in Texas in the same year as his diagnosis.

The third U.S. patient with vCJD was born and raised in Saudi Arabia and has lived permanently in the United States only since late 2005. According to the U.S. case report, the patient was most likely infected as a child when living in Saudi Arabia.[4]

As the recorded death toll for animals and people made clear that there were potential risks, the U.S. regulatory authorities undertook a series of preventive actions. Figure 5.4 provides the timeline for these efforts. In 1989 the USDA's Animal and Plant Health Inspection Service (APHIS) banned the importation of ruminant animals from the U.K.

[3]The Center for Infectious Disease Research and Policy (2005) observed: "The patient is a 30-year-old man who has lived in Houston for the past 4 years, according to an Associated Press (AP)... Born in the United Kingdom, the man lived there from 1980 until 1996, a period when residents were at risk for exposure to BSE-infected beef products, the AP reported."

[4]See National Creutzfeldt–Jakob Disease Research & Surveillance Unit (2013).

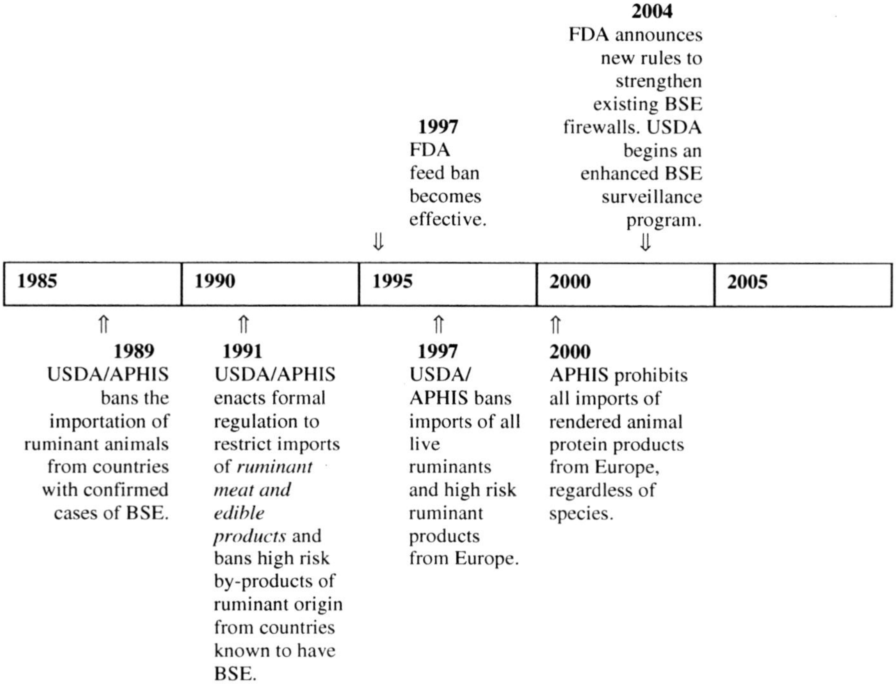

Fig. 5.4 U.S. policy actions.

and other countries with confirmed cases of BSE (21 C.F.R. §589.2000, 1997). Even before the 1989 policy went into effect, the U.S. had not been a major importer of cattle from the U.K. so there was no substantial U.S. exposure to BSE-infected cattle from the U.K. From 1981 through July 1989, the U.S. had only imported 334 cattle from the U.K. (Cohen et al., 2001). The USDA/APHIS extended these requirements in 1991 by enacting regulations that restricted imports of ruminant meat and edible products and banned high risk by-products of ruminant origin from countries known to have BSE. Two government agencies took action in 1997. The FDA feed ban became effective, and the USDA/APHIS banned imports of all live ruminants and high risk ruminant products from Europe.

The most important U.S. policy action was the 1997 feed ban that prohibited animal proteins in animal feed (21 C.F.R. §589.2000, 1997).

The FDA issued this rule because epidemiologic evidence based on the British BSE experience suggested that the BSE outbreak was due to ruminant feed containing animal protein derived from mammalian tissues. Moreover, the vCJD cases reported in the U.K. indicated a human risk from BSE. The underlying rationales for the rule consequently were based on the FDA's ability to observe the U.K. experience and to enact pertinent preventive measures.

Despite being a major rule, the FDA provided little by way of an assessment of the regulatory impacts. How great are the risks being prevented? The FDA did not even attempt a systematic risk analysis: "FDA explained that it could not develop an overall quantitative estimate of these benefits, primarily because it could not adequately measure the first of these factors, the probability that BSE would otherwise occur in the United States. While the agency determined that the risk was positive, the available data were inadequate to develop a quantitative risk assessment" (21 C.F.R. §589.2000, 1997, p. 30967).

Instead, the FDA presented a cost estimate based on a replication of the U.K. BSE outbreak in the U.S. That approach led to a cost estimate of \$3.8 billion due to protective measures such as destruction of livestock. Additional costs to consumers and lost market values were estimated to be in the "billions of dollars" as well (21 C.F.R. §589.2000, 1997, p. 30967). The cost of human lives lost is in addition to this amount.

The annual net feed-related costs of the rule were estimated to be \$52.9 million (21 C.F.R. §589.2000, 1997). These costs are net costs that take into account the gains to nonruminant feed sectors, which largely offset the meat and bone meal revenue loss. Additional annual costs of recordkeeping and labeling were estimated to be \$1.5 million to \$1.8 million annually (21 C.F.R. §589.2000, 1997).

With regulatory costs of about \$55 million annually and the cost of a BSE outbreak in excess of \$4 billion, the comparison of benefits and costs would appear to be clear-cut. However, at a 3 percent discount rate, annual costs of \$54 million indefinitely have a present value of \$1.8 billion. And it is noteworthy that the BSE outbreak costs assumed a replication of the U.K. experience. If, because of other differences between the two countries, the risk of a BSE outbreak is only 1/2 or

1/100, then the comparisons become quite different. How large must the risk be for expected benefits to exceed costs? The main problem is not that the FDA made the wrong decision by enacting the feed ban but rather that they did so without undertaking a more comprehensive risk analysis. Without comprehensively comparing the costs and the benefits it is not possible to ensure that the correct decisions have been made. This shortfall in regulatory analysis practices will be more consequential with respect to other policy actions related to BSE in which government agencies acted more based on hunches rather than analysis and did not always adopt the most protective policy approach.

While the FDA feed ban policy has been quite effective, it is less restrictive than the 1998 U.K. feed ban in that some ruminant proteins, such as milk and blood, are permitted in animal feed (Fox and Peterson, 2004). Unlike other countries that have enacted feed bans, the U.S. ban permits cattle feed to contain proteins from horses and pigs (U.S. GAO, 2002). Thus, assuming that the FDA feed ban would prevent a BSE outbreak appears to have been a strong assumption. In 2005, the FDA proposed a bolstering of the feed ban to eliminate many of the previous exceptions.[5]

Even after implementing the feed ban, the FDA was criticized by the U.S. General Accounting Office on several dimensions (U.S. GAO, 2002). The FDA lacked data to determine firms' compliance status with respect to the regulation. Follow-up inspections were also weak, as firms found to be out of compliance were not reinspected for two or more years. As with other regulatory programs, the hypothesized efficacy of the regulation is not borne out in practice.[6]

In 2004, the FDA announced new rules to strengthen existing BSE firewalls.[7] The USDA began an enhanced BSE surveillance program as

[5] Substances Prohibited from Use in Animal Food or Feed: Proposed Rule, 70 Fed. Reg. 58569 (Oct. 6, 2005) (to be codified at 21 CFR §589.1).

[6] Subsequent performance improved, but shortfalls remained. See U.S. GAO (2005).

[7] Other policy actions did, of course, follow. In January 2005, APHIS published a rule restricting ruminant imports. In March 2005, APHIS published a notice delaying the applicability of certain provisions of that rule. See Southeast Farm Press (2007). In January 2007, USDA/APHIS proposed a rule to expand imports from countries believed to be exporting meat of minimal risk. Also in 2007, there was an FDA proposal to restrict use of materials from cattle in medical products. See 72 Fed. Reg. 1582 (Jan. 12, 2007).

well, but phased it down to a less-extensive monitoring program after an assessment that BSE poses an "extremely low level of risk in the United States" (USDA, 2008a).

Another element of the BSE risk management regime that has received considerable attention in 2008 is the inspection of cattle at slaughter operations. The massive recall of beef products from the Westland/Hallmark meatpacking facility resulted from violation of inspection rules aimed at preventing downer cows from entering the food chain. So-called downer cows — animals that are not ambulatory — are more likely to be infected with BSE than ambulatory cattle. The Humane Society of the United States (HSUS) reports that 13 of the 16 BSE-infected cows identified in North America were downer cows (Pacelle, 2008).

To address this high-risk population, the USDA banned all downer cattle from the human food chain a week after the 2003 Washington BSE infection event (Pacelle, 2008). In January 2004, USDA announced an interim final rule to exclude downer cows from the food supply regardless of the reason for the nonambulatory status (Food Safety and Inspection Service (FSIS), 2004). Wayne Pacelle, the President of HSUS, explained the rationale for banning downers: "Since BSE can result in an animal going down either directly, because of brain damage, or indirectly, by predisposing an animal to injury, these downed cattle were to be euthanized rather than slaughtered for human consumption" (Pacelle, 2008, p. 39).

In apparent contrast to the plain language of the interim final rule, USDA provided guidance to inspecting veterinarians to allow downer cows into the human food supply if they appeared healthy other than for an acute injury that triggered their nonambulatory status (FSIS, 2004). The USDA incorporated this exception in the July 2007 regulation that made the ban on downer cows permanent (Pacelle, 2008).

Despite the presence of eight USDA inspectors at the Hallmark/Westland meatpacking facility (Boyle, 2008), the regulation requiring inspection of downer cows was violated. The HSUS undercover investigation demonstrated the ease with which workers could evade scrutiny by these inspectors who work full-time on site. The USDA's response has included a suspension of Hallmark/Westland as a supplier to government nutrition programs, like the school lunch program for which Hallmark/Westland was the number two supplier in the nation; suspension of inspection efforts by the Food Safety and Inspection Service (FSIS), which effectively shuts the facility down; and coordination of efforts to facilitate the beef recall (Schafer, 2008).

Almost invariably the regulatory impact analyses accompanying regulations pertaining to BSE and vCJD risks address consequences related to costs but do little to address benefits. The failure of the feed ban analysis to analyze reduced risks in a systematic and comprehensive manner is the norm for BSE policies.[8] Similarly, there is an exclusive cost focus of the 1996, 1997, and 2000 analyses of regulations to reduce risks from transmissible spongiform encephalopathies (TSE), including BSE, scrapie in sheep, and chronic wasting disease in mule deer and elk, among other diseases (Eastern Research Group, 1997, 1999, 2005a, 2005b). The 2001 trade association analysis of feeding regulations likewise focused on the cost effects rather than the effect of these regulations on the risks associated with feed (Sparks Company, 2001). This neglect of risk reduction benefits is more plausible from the standpoint of analyses on behalf of renderers than it would be for the meat industry generally or for analyses purporting to capture effects on the entire economy. One would expect trade associations to narrow the focus of their contribution to the policy debate to those issues of greatest pertinence to that group and matters where the association has some specialized expertise.

The 2005 USDA analysis of the emergency actions taken in response to the 2003 BSE-infected cow in Washington state similarly had a strong cost-based emphasis (FSIS, 2005). This report, however, drew on the 2001 Harvard–Tuskegee study of U.S. risks (Cohen et al., 2001) and their subsequent 2003 study of the risks to the U.S. from Canadian beef (Cohen and Gray, 2003). The Food Safety and Inspection Service also prepared simulations that modified the assumptions of the earlier studies. Moreover, unlike previous assessments, this study also undertakes quantitative risk assessments for the different policy alternatives. These are commendable improvements. What the study did

[8] See also the Center for Veterinary Medicine (1996).

not do is analyze the effect of reduced uncertainty regarding BSE risks on consumer welfare. Nor did the study attempt to monetize the health improvements in terms of reduced morbidity and mortality risks (e.g., with estimates of the value of statistical life).[9] What remains absent from such evaluations is a detailed comparison of the present value of the benefits and costs of the regulation.

[9] See Viscusi and Aldy (2003) for a review of the value of statistical life literature.

6

Media and Risk Communication

In situations of emerging risk information in which there is the potential for protective behavior by the public, including both producers and consumers, risk communication can play a potentially constructive role. Protective behavior by some consumers may include, for example, altering the types of foods that they eat to those that they perceive to pose a lower risk of BSE infectivity and therefore the transmission of vCJD. People other than consumers may take precautionary actions on behalf of consumers, such as by filtering blood used for transfusions to remove the vCJD prions. For risk information to serve a constructive role, ideally it should provide an accurate characterization of the risk level. Doing so in situations in which the scientific community and the government also do not know the precise nature of the risk remains a challenging enterprise. As indicated above, people will tend to treat situations of risk ambiguity as if they posed a known risk that is greater than the average expected risk level. Thus, if the government provides risk information that reflects the uncertainty that is present with respect to the level of the risk, there may tend to be an alarmist response. However, if the government misrepresents the risk level or claims to have more precise or less precise knowledge than it does, then the government runs the risk of undermining its credibility in future contacts with the public. Perhaps in part because of the difficulties posed by the mad cow risk communication experience, it is noteworthy that in the European literature on risk management, the role of trust plays a much more prominent role than it does in the U.S. literature on risk analysis.[1]

The retrospective assessment of how well the risks were communicated to the public has not been favorable. The chair of the U.K. government's advisory committee on spongiform encephalopathy diseases made the following observations in 2007 about the BSE outbreak: "The politicians did not know what to do and the scientists did not know what to do. We didn't know where it came from, what caused it, how bad it might be. We didn't know anything" (Sample, 2007).

In such situations of risk ignorance one might have expected a cautious government response that might preserve the government's credibility should the disease spread to humans. Instead, the government's chief medical officer, Sir Donald Acheson, declared that beef was safe to eat, and then Agricultural Minister, John Gummer, fed a hamburger on camera to his four-year-old daughter in an apparent effort to persuade the British public of the beef's safety (Sample, 2007; Weintraub, 2004). Even the BSE working party headed by Sir Richard Southwood concluded in 1989 that it was "most unlikely BSE would have any implications for human health" (Sample, 2007). The risk communication message of reassurance lacked credibility (Sample, 2007). There is a general belief that the British government's risk communication regarding the mad cow risks were biased by a desire to protect the British cattle industry and to foster political interests rather than to protect consumer welfare (Lanska, 1998).

More generally, the entire policy response is viewed by some as an abject failure. As van Zwanenberg and Millstone (2005) conclude in their treatise on the U.K. BSE crisis: "The BSE saga that began in the mid-1980s (and which continues to this day) represents the worst failure of U.K. public policy since the Suez adventure of 1956, when measured in terms of the economic, political, and diplomatic harm that it caused"

[1] See Löfstedt (2005) for discussion of trust in the context of European risk management.

(p. 4). The authors hypothesize that the failure to undertake a risk analysis was due in part to "avoid perturbing agricultural markets" (van Zwanenberg and Millstone, 2005, p. 71).

Before the emergence of vCJD in humans, there was some disagreement in the scientific community as to the potential for this disease to cross the species barrier. At one extreme, scientists such as scrapie expert Richard Marsh, who was a Professor of Veterinary Science at the University of Wisconsin, declared: "I don't think there's any risk to humans" (Cherfas, 1990, p. 1492). This skepticism regarding the possible link to humans was also shared by a U.K. Working Group of the Committee of Safety of Medicines, which in 1989 referred to the risk to humans as being "remote" (van Zwanenberg and Millstone, 2005, p. 110). The contrary view was not that there was a human risk but simply that we didn't know yet if there was a risk. Heino Deringer of the Robert Koch Institute in Berlin expressed a more generic view: "We do not know if [the disease] will change in cattle. We cannot assume that because [eating] sheep is relatively safe, ergo beef is safe" (van Zwanenberg and Millstone, 2005, p. 110).

By 1995 there would be the start of recorded vCJD fatalities in the U.K., and shortly thereafter in March of 1996, the British government announced the human linkage. Some observers speculated that the industry and government colluded to suppress the fears of vCJD, where these fears were especially pronounced among parents of small children (Bellaby, 2003). The public's perceptions were grounded in a distrust of the food industry, skepticism regarding public health authorities' ability to regulate the industry, and a disbelief of government officials who made the incredulous claim that beef posed no public health risk (Wall, 2007).

The British press added to the public's sense of alarm:

> Britain's National Euthanasia Clinics [will] churn on overtime, struggling to help 500 people a week to a dignified death before brain disease robs them of reason and self-control. This nation, whose leaders spent a decade in denial, [will be] quarantined, the world having long since shunned contact with a population

> in which half a million people a year succumb to Creutzfeldt-Jakob disease, a fatal neurological illness spread... through the eating of infected beef products. The Channel Tunnel [will be] blocked with five miles of French concrete. The health service [will be] crippled; blood transfusions [will be] impossible because undetectable prions — the cause of the disease — infect most donors and the strain of caring for more than two million CJD victims [will overwhelm] support staff. The fabric of the nation [will be] torn apart (Lanska, 1998, p. 170).[2]

In *Today* newspaper (U.K.), March 1, 1990, Professor Richard Lacey was quoted as saying that due to BSE, "in years to come our hospitals will be filled with thousands of people going slowly and painfully mad before dying" (Phillips et al., 2000, Volume 6, Chapter 4, Paragraph 4.479, p. 348).

The risk ambiguity debate also undermined the credibility of the scientific community. Only 19 percent of the population reported that the establishment of the BSE link from cattle to humans improved the image of science, while 33 percent believed that the image has suffered greatly.[3] The public was almost equally divided as to whether scientists have been used by politicians (29 percent), scientists have caused a scare without understanding what is going on (27 percent), and scientists are unreliable (21 percent).

The diffuseness of the risk estimates from the scientific community was sufficiently great as to serve no constructive role other than to alert people to a possible hazard that might even be enormous. In 1997, two years after the first confirmed vCJD death, Cousens et al. (1997) predicted a few hundred to many thousands (around 13,000 infections) of vCJD.[4] One scientist in 1996 estimated that the number

[2] Note that Lanska quotes from R. McKie et al., (1996), 'A conspiracy to drive us all mad'. *Observer* March 24, p. 16.

[3] The Gallup Org., Gallup Poll, England, Sept. 1996.

[4] Cousens et al.'s (1997) estimated numbers reflect the extreme sensitivity of the results to the shape of the incubation period distribution, its mean and its variability. The

of British deaths would be from 500 to 500,000 (*The Economist*, 1996).[5] The estimates by Thomas and Newly (1999) were published despite "disagreement among the referees regarding the quality of the paper," but produced a relatively low vCJD case estimate that "is predicted not to exceed a few hundred, and is most likely to be a hundred or less." At the lower end of the prediction spectrum, Brown et al. (2001) estimated an annual number of vCJD cases of 10–15 beginning in 1994.

In 2000, Oxford scientists led by epidemiologist Roy Anderson revised their earlier vCJD estimate of 500,000 cases, which is almost 1 percent of the entire 1996 U.K. population, to a maximum of 136,000 deaths (Balter, 2000). Even this estimate will prove to be several orders of magnitude too large. Adopting a more realistic incubation period than the 60-year period that led to the 136,000 case estimate leads to an estimate of the maximum number of cases equal to about 10,000 (Balter, 2000). Other scientists were reluctant to make any projections until after the incidence of vCJD reached a peak and started to decline (Balter, 2000).

Estimates of the vCJD infection rate by Huillard d'Aignaux et al. (2001) indicated that while the estimated number of cases probably would not be more than "a few thousand," the estimated range of possible cases was from a few hundred to an epidemic affecting millions.

A principal reason for the substantial uncertainty is that the estimates are very sensitive to the assumed incubation period. Estimates in 2003 of the total number of vCJD cases in the U.K. range from "a few hundred to several million" (Huillard d'Aignaux et al., 2003). However, this upper bound estimate requires an incubation period that likely

assumptions about the effect of varying the assumptions about incubation period were the greatest observed.

[5] The 500,000 estimate is, however, an outlier. As noted by Lanska (1998), "Assuming that, despite all of the above, BSE could be transmitted to humans with high infectivity, Britain could find itself with 500,000 or more human cases per year of a fatal neurodegenerative illness resembling CJD.... Despite the authoritative pronouncements and scientific rationale to the contrary, this last scenario (with 500,000 or more human cases per year of CJD) has been considered a 'wholly feasible future for Britain' by many of the public, by some of the media, and by a few counter-establishment scientists" (p. 169).

extends past the normal expected lifetime. More realistic incubation period estimates suggest a maximum number of vCJD cases in the U.K. of several thousand (Huillard d'Aignaux et al., 2003). Incorporation of age distribution variations in the risk into earlier models developed by other researchers led Valleron et al. (2001) to estimate predictions of 80 to 630 cases based on the Ghani model and 801 based on the Cousens model. A more realistic set of estimates of the vCJD toll in 2003 pegged the total number of deaths at between 183 and 204 (Böelle et al., 2003). Estimates in 2003 by Ghani et al. (2003) ruled out the possibility of a large number of vCJD diagnoses in the next 5 to 10 years but highlighted the continued future uncertainty.

Risk ranges that differ by a factor of 1,000 reflect enormous imprecision in knowledge. Among the factors influencing the span of estimates, as noted by Cousens et al. (1997), include the unknown degree of underreporting of BSE cases, the degree of effectiveness of the feed bans, and the length of the incubation period.

Predicting the ultimate number of vCJD cases is quite different as it requires assumptions about the level of exposure and the incubation period about which little may be known. Even within a single study there may be a broad range of estimates depending on the assumptions on which the calculations are based.

With only 177 deaths in the U.K. through November 2013 and just over 200 documented cases worldwide, these estimates are surely far off the mark. While there might well be a substantial incubation period, the temporal distribution of the deaths in the U.K., where exposures to BSE began two decades ago, suggests that the incubation period is not so long that there is any chance that these risk estimates might be borne out.

Individuals have a tendency to overreact to newly identified hazards in products for which they have an accustomed risk level. In situations where a product was formerly viewed as safe, the disruption in people's previous sense of the magnitude of the risk often generates an overreaction to the risk level that prevails after the risk increase. Thus, consumers tend to focus not on the actual level of the new risk, but rather they react in an extreme way to the fact that there has been an identification of a new risk and an increase in the risk from its previous level.[6] How people reacted to the mad cow crisis is one of the best documented market responses to changes in the reference risk level, as most previous studies of the phenomenon were based on survey responses and experimental scenarios.

What is especially noteworthy about the mad cow experience is that some members of the scientific community may have overreacted as well. It may well be, of course, that the more extreme estimates of the death toll from vCJD received the most coverage, but other than the government's early disavowal of a substantial risk to people, the risk estimates that were publicized predicted mass carnage from vCJD. These wildly excessive risk estimates may not have been borne out because of the aggressive measures undertaken in the U.K. to address the risk. But even after most of these policies were in place, there were still predictions of a death toll many orders of magnitude greater than the actual number of fatalities. In contrast, information provided by the government was consistently less dire than the worst case scenarios that received press attention.

A principal mechanism by which risk information is communicated is through the media. We employed a LexisNexis search engine to monitor U.S. media coverage on BSE and vCJD over the 1986–2005 period.[7] The period from 1986 through 1995 witnessed the emergence of coverage of BSE risks in the U.S. Sample (2007) notes that "Without publicity, an investigation was launched [in the U.K.] to find the cause of the outbreak. It revealed an alarmingly widespread disease. One year later, 95 cases of BSE had been confirmed on 80 farms." From 1986 to 1988 there was no press coverage in the sources above, thus

[6] Gayer et al. (2000) show how information about the listing of hazardous waste sites on the Superfund National Priorities List initially results in large reductions in the value of nearby homes. As more information about the cancer risks associated with the Superfund sites are released through the official Remedial Investigation, the home market prices recover substantially. The initial "over-reaction" yielded an estimated value for avoiding a statistical cancer case approximately ten times the value estimated for residents after release of the additional risk information.

[7] In particular, we focused on full text articles obtained from the LexisNexis Major U.S. Newspapers Database. This Major U.S. Newspapers source contains English language newspapers published in the U.S. that are listed in the top 50 in circulation in the Editor & Publisher Year Book. The search terms that we used were as follows: ALLCAPS(BSE) OR (BOVINE SPONGIFORM ENCEPHALOPATHY!) OR (MAD COW!). The search criteria specified were: January 1, 1986–December 31, 2005.

establishing the reference point before the risks became publicized. By 1990 the number of articles [in the U.S.] related to the BSE events in the U.K. increased to 25, and there was a consistent level of 10–25 articles annually from 1990 to 1995. The article topics spanned a wide range including trade disputes in the EU regarding exports of beef, the toll of more than 10,000 cattle killed by the disease in Britain, new research on the spread of disease through cattle feed, and statements by the U.K. government that there appears to be only a remote risk to humans.

The media frenzy began on March 21–22, 1996 with 56 media stories within two days following the U.K. government's announcement of the apparent link between BSE and humans. From 1996 to 2005 there was close to daily coverage of the disease in the U.S. media. Particularly heavy news coverage occurred in 2003 and 2004 after the USDA announced the first and second cases of BSE in the U.S.

The dramatic effect of the announced link to humans in 1996 occurred 10 years after the disease in animals was discovered in Britain. One would expect this surge in media coverage to lead to an increase in U.S. public consciousness with respect to the disease, which will be examined below. Part of the surge in public awareness can be attributed to what might be called the "Oprah effect." There were more than 100 media stories that referenced Oprah Winfrey's show on April 16, 1996 dealing with mad cow disease. The knowledge of the human link between vCJD and the extensive public concern perhaps influenced the timing of the FDA's 1997 Feed Ban. In January 1997, the rule was proposed, in June 1997 the rule was issued, and in August 1997 the feed ban rule became effective.

The extent of publicity for BSE-related information also carried over to studies that provided more reassuring news. The Harvard/Tuskegee risk assessment in Cohen et al. (2001) received coverage in 15 major newspapers. The bottom line of the study indicated a low human risk in the U.S.: "In summary, measures taken by the U.S. government and industry make the U.S. robust against the spread of BSE to animals or humans should it be introduced to this country." (Cohen et al., 2001). This study substantially advanced government analysis of BSE but is based on an assumption of consistent conditions over time (Harvard Center for Risk Analysis and Center for Computational

Epidemiology, 2002). New conditions, such as the development of new testing protocols, lie outside the model.

The February 2008 major recall of beef products from the Westland/Hallmark meat-packing facility provides a challenge for risk communication. The recall of 143 million pounds of beef products have been designed as Class II recall, which has a "remote probability" that the recalled products could result in adverse health effects (USDA, 2008b). The recall designation reflects the fact that a violated inspection protocol — failure to notify the USDA veterinarian on-site of a downer cow prior to slaughter — and not detection of BSE contamination occurred. The issue has been especially salient in the media because some 37 million pounds of recalled beef had been distributed to public schools through the USDA's School Lunch Program. A substantial number of stories in local print and television media addressed the question of whether schools in their cities received meat through this program.[8] Efforts to reassure the public about the safety of the food supply by USDA have been challenged by the editorial pages of several leading newspapers,[9] and may have overreached what evidence can support. For example, several media reports indicated that government officials have noted that no one has gotten sick from eating the beef.[10] Representatives of the meat-packing industry have emphasized this claim, as illustrated in Congressional testimony by J. Patrick Boyle, President of the American Meat Institute: "Federal officials have said that the beef supply is safe and there have been no illnesses associated with the recalled meat" (Boyle, 2008, p. 52). Given the multiple year incubation period for vCJD, one should not have expected symptomatic cases at that time.

---

[8] For example, a simple Google News search of all of the words in the phrase "beef recall schools" generates more than 3,500 news stories for the week of February 16–22. For examples of such stories, refer to Jones (2008), Kim and Wilson (2008), and Vargas (2008).

[9] Examples of editorials on the beef recall include those in major city newspapers such as the *New York Times* (Feb. 21, 2008), and the *Baltimore Sun* (Feb. 21, 2008), as well as those in smaller city papers such as the *Sarasota Herald-Tribune* (Feb. 20, 2008) and the *Bismarck Tribune* (Feb. 21, 2008).

[10] A CNN online story states: "Keith Williams, a U.S. Department of Agriculture spokesman, said investigators have found no cases of illness related to the recalled meat" (CNN, 'USDA orders recall of 143 million pounds of beef.' Feb. 18, 2008, available at http://www.cnn.com/2008/HEALTH/02/17/beef.recall/, last visited Nov. 14, 2013.) See also Jones (2008).

7

Consumer Responses to the Mad Cow Crisis

The first measure of consumer responses that we examine is public opinion polls. To what extent has the media coverage led to awareness of BSE and vCJD risks, and if there is awareness, do consumers believe that there is a risk to themselves? In addition, how satisfied are they with how the government has handled the mad cow risk threat?

In 1995 and in early 1996, two different U.K. polls indicated that substantial percentages of the population (45 percent and 52 percent) were very worried or somewhat worried about the possible spread of the disease to humans.[1] These concerns in turn were reflected in consumers' stated consumption decisions: they reduced the level and composition of their beef eating.[2] The worry about the risks was coupled with a lack of trust in the government. Overall, 70 percent of the British public in

[1] Gallup Poll, England, Dec. 1995; Gallup Poll, England, Apr. 1996.

[2] Overall, 22 percent of respondents reported eating fewer beef products like sausages and beefburgers, and 7 percent stopped eating beef products entirely. An additional 6 percent were vegetarian. (Gallup England, Dec. 1995.) The Apr. 1996 Gallup England poll reported that with respect to cuts of beef such as steak and roast beef, 17 percent ate fewer cuts of beef, 10 percent stopped eating beef entirely, and 7 percent were vegetarian. Also in Apr. 1996, for beef products such as sausages and hamburgers, 25 percent stopped eating beef products, and 31 percent ate fewer beef products.

1995 thought that the government was withholding some facts about BSE, and only 14 percent believed the Ministry of Agriculture, Fisheries and Food was keeping the public fully informed.[3] Ninety percent of the public believed the government was withholding some facts.[4] The worry and distrust did not abate after the government announced the link in March 1996. An astounding 86 percent of the respondents in 1996 indicated that they were "suspicious" of what the Ministers have to say.[5] Similarly, three 1996 U.K. polls indicated that the government had handled the BSE problems pretty badly or very badly, with 70 percent and 82 percent expressing such displeasure.[6]

The opinion polls in the U.S. likewise indicate a concern with the disease. In 2001, 65 percent of respondents indicated that they were very concerned or somewhat concerned about mad cow disease becoming a problem in the U.S.[7] By 2004, 16 percent of those interviewed indicated that they were very worried or somewhat worried that someone in their family would become a victim of mad cow disease.[8] This expression of concern for a within family risk is extremely high relative to the actual risk level. More people in the U.S. die every 15 minutes in traffic accidents than have died in any year from vCJD.[9] Even the worst case estimate of what the vCJD risk might be in the U.K. had about 1 out of 100 in the population dying, and the actual death toll reflects a total death risk of under 3 per million people.

Unlike in the U.K., there is a much greater expression of trust in government among the U.S. population. In 2004, 45 percent of respondents indicated a great deal of trust in the government's handling of the mad cow risks, and an additional 43 percent indicated that they were somewhat confident in the government.[10] It may be, of course, that the actions by the government in the U.S. were not necessarily

[3] An additional 16 percent were recorded as "don't know." Gallup England, Dec. 1995.
[4] Gallup Poll, England, Apr. 1996.
[5] Gallup Poll, England, Apr. 1996.
[6] Gallup Poll, England, Jul. 1996; Gallup Poll, England, Apr. 1996; Gallup Poll, England, Jun. 1996. Similarly, 69 percent of European Union residents agreed that politicians bear a great deal of responsibility for the mad cow disease affair. Eurobarometer, Dec. 2001.
[7] CNN/USA Today/Gallup Poll, Mar. 22, 2001.
[8] CNN/USA Today/Gallup Poll, Jan. 9, 2004.
[9] These calculations draw on data from the National Safety Council (2007).
[10] *Wall Street Journal* (2004).

sounder than those undertaken in the U.K. because the U.S. never had to deal with a BSE outbreak after it had occurred. Rather, the U.S. was fortunate in that the government was not dealing with an actual BSE crisis, whereas the U.K was. It is conceivable that in countries in which there has never been a BSE case that people might express confidence in the government even though the good record for mad cow disease may have nothing whatsoever to do with actions taken by the government.

Expressions of consumer concern should, of course, also be reflected in their consumption decisions. If eating beef poses risks of vCJD that have just become identified, then that will decrease the attractiveness of eating beef relative to other less risky foods, whether it be chicken or vegetarian options. Similarly, if people are to continue to eat beef, then in the same manner that safer cars command a price premium, safer beef will do so as well.

The first set of evidence on this phenomenon is not based on actual purchases but on consumers' stated preferences with respect to what they are willing to pay. The survey context is Japan, where the first BSE-infected cow was found in September 2001. In December 2001, a contingent valuation study undertaken in Nagano examined consumer preferences at a convenience sample of 381 shoppers at a food cooperative (McCluskey et al., 2005).[11] Japanese consumers indicated that they would be willing to pay a 50 percent price premium for beef labeled as BSE tested. The substantial effect of the BSE risk on willingness to pay is quite consistent with the observed quantity effect. After a third infected cow was identified within a three-month period, beef consumption in Japan had fallen by nearly 70 percent. The study by Jin and Koo (2003) found that the decline in consumer demand for beef was due to a post-BSE structural change in beef demand. It took more than three years for beef demand in Japan to return to its pre-BSE event market share (Ishida et al., 2010). Understanding of the quite prominent concerns with BSE risks among Japanese consumers also

[11] The study had a 50 percent response rate and used a referendum elicitation of willingness-to-pay for BSE tested beef. The payment vehicle for measuring willingness-to-pay was the price for tested beef.

may help put into context the subsequent Japanese ban on U.S. beef imports after the identification of an infected animal in the U.S.

Beef consumption also declined in countries following the 1996 U.K. announcement of a vCJD risk to humans. Burton and Young (1996, 1997) found that in the U.S. the beef share of the meat market declined 4–5 percent as pork and lamb shares increased. Following the U.K. announcement, consumption of beef in France fell by 30 percent as shown in the detailed analysis by Adda (2007). The change in consumption varied across the population. Adda found that households with little historic beef consumption did not statistically reduce consumption. Likewise, those households with relatively high rates of beef consumption failed to meaningfully reduce their beef consumption, providing evidence of habit formation. The households spanning the middle of the beef consumption distribution undertook the most significant (in economic and statistical terms) reductions in beef consumption.

Spanish consumption of beef declined by nearly one-fifth in the year after the November 2000 identification of BSE-infected cows in Spain. Within about a year, domestic consumption returned to pre-2000 levels. Producer prices responded (negatively) more than retail prices in Spain, and the response was more pronounced during periods of greater news coverage (Hassouneh et al., 2010).

The response in the U.S. after the announcement of a BSE-infected cow in 2003 was less pronounced. Kuchler and Tegene (2006) found a short-lived, modest reduction in beef consumption, while Schlenker and Villas-Boas (2009) found a 25–30 percent transitory reduction. In both empirical analyses of U.S. beef consumption, the estimated response to the new BSE risk information dissipated quickly so that beef consumption returned to pre-announcement levels within a few months. This substantial immediate but brief reaction may reflect a large, initial subjective probability of consuming BSE-infected beef. Over the subsequent weeks, consumers updated their perceived probability of risk exposure in light of the absence of additional findings of infected cows. Eventually, the revised subjective probabilities converged toward the pre-announcement assessment of risk, and beef consumption increased.

In May 2003, Canada reported its first case of mad cow disease. Cattle prices fell by nearly half in the first three months after this case, while retail beef prices declined about 14 percent (Boame et al., 2004). Ding et al. (2011) find an immediate but temporary reduction in beef consumption in their analysis of household meat expenditure data among Canadian consumers. Their analysis also presents some evidence of habit formation and consumption persistence, which may mitigate behavioral response to new risk information.

U.S. consumers also would be willing to pay more for red meat that had a farm-to-slaughter traceability system much like that required throughout the European Union (Dickinson and Bailey, 2005). Among the very few private firms that instituted traceable meat product systems is Creekstone Farms (Dickinson and Bailey, 2005), which will also be the most prominent producer in the BSE testing controversy described below.

As one might expect given the nature of economic markets, the decreased consumer demand for beef had ramifications for cattle futures markets as well. Schlenker and Villas-Boas (2009) found that futures prices fell by about 20 percent after the identification of a BSE-infected cow in 2003. Following a pattern similar to that in the consumer market, futures prices recovered within a three-month period. Moreover, the 2003 BSE cases in Canada and the United States increased price volatility, especially for nearby maturities, in the cattle futures market for about three months after the reports of infected cows (Jin et al., 2008).[12] This reflects the learning of a new, unexpected risk in beef markets and an eventual assessment that the risks, as perceived by consumers, appear to be modest.

[12] Spanish producer and retail prices also experienced increased volatility after the first announced BSE cases in Spain in November 2000, with greater volatility in producer prices than in retail prices (Serra, 2011).

8

Trade Bans and Country-of-Origin Labeling Policies

Governments responded to information about mad cow risks in trade partners typically by imposing at least short-term prohibitions on imports from countries announcing BSE-infected cattle. The U.S. imposed a ban on imports of cattle products from the U.K. in 1989 and the European Union followed suit with an import ban in 1996. In 1997, after mounting evidence of BSE and vCJD in Europe, the U.S. banned imports from all EU countries (Gray et al., 2011). In 2003, the U.S. banned imports from Canada after the government in Ottawa announced the finding of the first BSE-infected cow. Japan, Korea, Mexico, and other countries banned imports from the U.S. after it reported its first BSE case in December 2003.

Such policy responses may reflect one or more factors. First, governments may ban imports reflecting the public's concern about the safety of imported beef or cattle, even if such concerns reflect a limited information base. Indeed, the strong preference for BSE-free beef in Japan discussed above, or the high premium for domestic beef in Korea (Chung et al., 2009) provides some basis for a ban.

Second, such a policy action may serve to protect domestic beef producers. Such a move may not be "protectionist" given the asymmetric information (or the symmetric and inadequate information) on beef safety and beef origins characterizing retail markets. Thus, if consumers cannot discern domestic beef from beef imported from a country with non-zero BSE risk, then they may pay less for all beef, or substitute to another good altogether. The import ban serves to support the claim (made by industry and likely the government) that the beef for sale within a domestic market is safe for consumption. Indeed, these concerns motivate another policy response addressed below: country-of-origin labeling. Of course, the case could also be made that domestic producers can leverage concerns about BSE to increase costs on or close markets to foreign competition.

Third, given the policy and communication errors of the U.K. government in the mid-1990s, political leaders in other countries have an incentive to take quick, clear action to mitigate the poorly known, if not unknown, risks of importing BSE-infected cattle and beef. An import policy is a relatively straightforward policy to implement and is easy to communicate.

Fourth, bans typically impose meaningful costs on cattle producers in exporting countries. As a result, an import ban may provide a tool for one government to leverage better food and animal safety policies and surveillance in other countries.

The import bans appear to have had a much longer and more substantial impact on cattle and beef producers than did changes in domestic consumption after the reporting of cases of BSE-infected cows. While U.S. beef consumption dropped modestly and rebounded in a matter of months after the December 2003 mad cow case (Schlenker and Villas-Boas, 2009; Kuchler and Tegene, 2006), U.S. weekly beef exports fell nearly 99 percent in two weeks and briefly returned to pre-December 2003 levels for only a short period of time nearly five years later in 2008 before the Great Recession decreased foreign demand (Figure 8.1). U.S. cattle producers received nearly 15 percent lower prices per head of cattle due to the prohibitions on exporting to Japan and Korea (Marsh et al., 2008). The bans reduced beef export revenues on the order of about \$3 billion (Tsigas et al., 2008). Mutondo et al. (2009) estimate that the import bans by Japan and Korea imposed losses on U.S. beef producers in excess of \$0.5 billion.

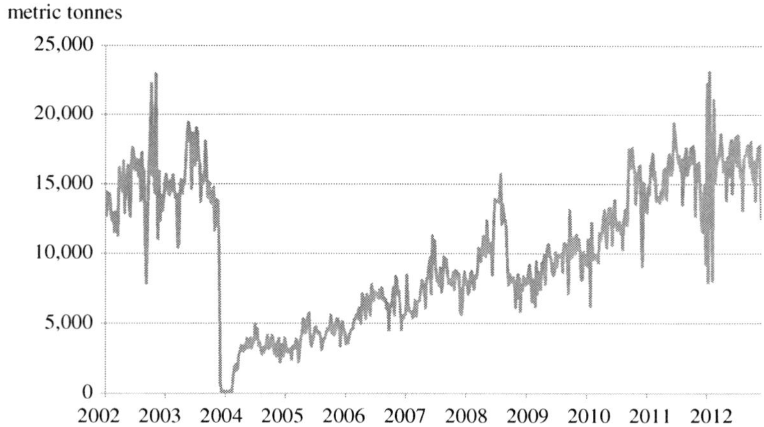

Fig. 8.1 Weekly U.S. beef exports, 2002–2012.

Source: USDA Foreign Agricultural Service Export Sales Reporting Internet Portal, available at http://www.fas.usda.gov/esrquery/esrq.aspx (last visited February 2, 2013). Data represent fresh, chilled, or frozen muscle cuts of beef.

Canada's annual beef export revenues to the U.S. fell by two-thirds in 2003 and 2004 after the announcement of its first BSE-infected cow case (Figure 8.2). Since Canadian beef comprised about three-quarters of U.S. beef imports, the ban on Canadian beef imposed meaningful costs on both countries. Producers in Canada witnessed a steep decline in cattle prices, and the aggregate losses to the Canadian economy were about $1 billion (Wigle et al., 2007). In a computable general equilibrium analysis of the ban on Canadian imports, Wieck and Holland (2010) show that the subsequent increase in domestic cattle prices (relative to the counterfactual) imposed a loss of about $1.7 billion to the U.S. economy.

In response to concerns about the adverse impacts of blunt instruments such as trade bans, governments explored other policy instruments, such as country-of-origin labeling. Country-of-origin labeling provides information that some consumers value, given estimated premia for domestic beef in U.S. and Korean markets (Lim et al., 2013; Chung et al., 2009). Of course, country-of-origin does not necessarily speak to the safety of or even the BSE risk of beef, in contrast to explicit beef testing (see the next section on this issue).

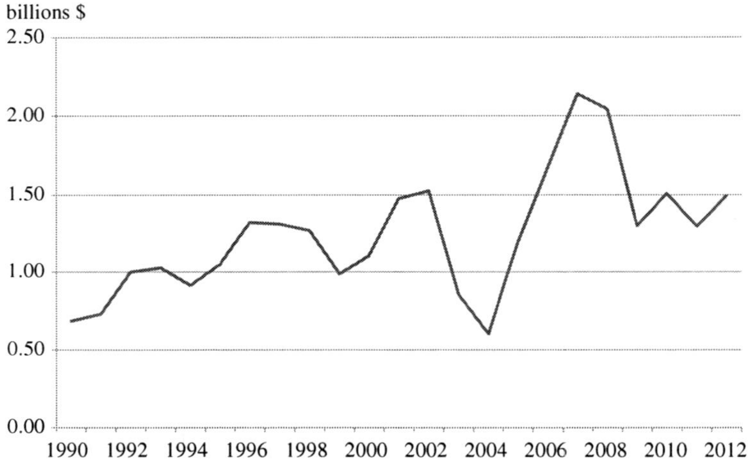

Fig. 8.2 Annual Canadian beef exports to the United States, 1990–2012.

Source: USDA Foreign Agricultural Service Global Agricultural Trade System Online, http://www.fas.usda.gov/gats/ExpressQuery1.aspx, (last accessed November 8, 2013).

Country-of-origin labeling establishes a surveillance regime that effectively permits the identification, tracking, and even traceability of individual heads of cattle throughout the cattle and beef production, processing, marketing, and retailing system. As a result, it can impose costs throughout the supply chain. For example, Jones et al. (2009) estimated that the operating costs would increase by about 1.3 percent for cattle suppliers and 2.1 to 2.2 percent for processors and retailers for the U.S. Country-of-Origin Labeling (COOL) regulation promulgated by the USDA in 2009. They find that such a labeling requirement reduces international trade, and absent a significant demand for labeled beef, would reduce consumer and producer welfare. Indeed, the USDA regulatory impact analysis summarized in the published rule shows an increase in beef prices and reductions in exports and imports.[1] It should also be noted that USDA makes no claims about food safety, including

[1] USDA "Mandatory Country of Origin Labeling of Beef, Pork, Lamb, Chicken, Goat, Meat, Wild and Farm-Raised Fish and Shellfish, Perishable Agricultural Commodities, Peanuts, Pecans, Ginseng, and Macadamia Nuts; Final Rule," 74 *Federal Register* 2670, January 15, 2009.

mitigating BSE risk, in its assessment of the benefits and costs of the COOL regulation.

Given the need to track and potentially separate cattle and beef by country-of-origin, one potential behavioral response for domestic processors and retailers would be to limit its sourcing to exclusively domestic suppliers, which could thereby reduce the costs of complying with the regulation. Out of concern for just such a response, Canada and Mexico challenged the U.S. COOL regulation before the World Trade Organization (Johnecheck, 2010). In a 2011 ruling and a 2012 appellate review, the WTO found that the U.S. regulation violated Article 2.1 of the Agreement on Technical Barriers to Trade, which requires WTO members to ensure that "products imported from the territory of any Members shall be accorded treatment no less favorable than that accorded to like products of national origin and to like products originating in any other country."

The USDA promulgated a 2013 revision to the regulation with the intent of complying with the WTO decision. Assuming the 2013 revision withstands any further WTO scrutiny, the outstanding policy question is whether COOL sufficiently informs consumers that it would preclude the need for an import ban in the event of a future BSE case (or potentially similar food-borne health risk).

9

The Testing Controversy

The identification of a cow infected with BSE in the state of Washington in December 2003 marked the advent of the mad cow problem in the U.S. Almost immediately, foreign countries banned the importation of U.S. beef.[1] The U.S. government also responded promptly, as the USDA undertook a much more extensive testing program than it had in the past through its general surveillance program. The Food Safety and Inspection Service of the USDA prohibited certain tissues from use in the human food chain, including the small intestine and brains of all cattle and the spinal cord and brains of cattle over 30 months old.[2] FSIS also prohibited downer cattle for human consumption.[3] The Animal and Plant Health Inspection Service of the USDA instituted increased testing of high-risk cattle. In June 2004, the USDA introduced the

[1] For general background regarding the events described below, see Viña (2006), Mathews, Jr. et al. (2006), and Lister and Becker (2007).

[2] These regulations are discussed in Robertson (2007).

[3] This is the cause for the largest beef recall in U.S. history announced in February 2008 by the Westland/Hallmark Meat Company. The Humane Society documented through undercover video that the company did not solicit USDA inspectors to evaluate downer cows at their slaughter facilities (Martin, 2008).

use of "rapid" immunologic test kits.[4] These "rapid tests" of samples of brain tissues provide evidence of abnormal BSE proteins within a few hours, as compared to the delay of up to two weeks for the more comprehensive immunohistochemistry test results. The combined cost of these regulations totaled about $200 million (Coffey et al., 2005a,b).

As extensive as these U.S. measures were, they fell short of the actions taken by other countries to protect their consumers. After Japan's first BSE case in 2001, beef consumption plummeted, and a mandatory testing program was instituted for all slaughtered animals irrespective of age (Normile, 2004). After the testing protocol was instituted, Japanese beef consumption recovered. Prohibiting U.S. imports that were not tested consequently was not a protectionist trade barrier but rather an effort to have imports meet the same standards as imposed on domestic beef.[5]

Almost immediately after the BSE-infected cow was identified in the U.S. in 2003, 53 countries including the second and third largest importers of U.S. beef, Japan and Korea, banned the importation of U.S. beef in the absence of a testing protocol for all cattle (Coffey et al., 2005a,b). In 2004 alone, the value of U.S. beef exports that were lost because of the bans totaled $3.2 billion to $4.7 billion (Fox et al., 2005). Analysis of the weekly U.S. beef exports to Japan indicates the drastic effect the ban had on U.S. exports. In the first week of January 2003, weekly exports were 3,941 metric tons.[6] This pace continued throughout the year at or above this level, and in the first week of December 2003, exports were 4,359 metric tons. After a drop in exports in the last week of 2003, exports declined to 204 metric tons in the first week of 2004 and never exceeded a value of 1 metric ton until December 2005. In that month, the U.S. reached an agreement with Japan to be able to export beef from cattle that were twenty months or younger. This

[4] Whereas the USDA uses the Bio-Rad rapid screening test, Europe and Japan use the Western Blot Test, which Consumers Union believes is more sensitive and objective than the Bio-Rad test (Bailey et al., 2005).

[5] Japanese consumers substituted Australian and New Zealand beef for U.S. beef (Lister and Becker, 2007).

[6] Beef export data are from USDA/FAS/Export Sales Reporting, Export Sales Query System, Export Sales Query Data by Commodity/Date, internet: http://www.fas.usda.gov/esrquery/esrq.aspx. Last accessed February 3, 2013.

improvement was short lived, as exports dropped to zero again before the end of January 2006.

In December 2005, the foreign market for U.S. meat was reopened only briefly before banned materials (bone) were found in a shipment of U.S. veal. After six months of negotiations, the market again reopened on July 26, 2006. The U.S. had a third indigenous BSE case in March 2006. At that point Japanese imports of U.S. beef were already at zero, so there was no effect on exports directly surrounding the event. Exports did not begin to recover until August 2006, but until 2008 exports remained well below their earlier levels and have only reached a value of 1,000 metric tons three times.

Given the dramatic effect that the BSE cases have had on U.S. exports, some beef producers sought to have their beef tested and labeled safe so as to be eligible for importation to Japan. The variable cost per head of such testing is about $15 to $20 (Coffey et al., 2005a,b).[7] While some producers favored voluntary testing, other producers feared that testing would be required generally by beef importers and opposed testing as an unnecessary and costly expense (Coffey et al., 2005a,b). The most prominent of these testing programs was that launched by Creekstone Farms Premium Beef. That company is a specialty producer and processor of Black Angus Beef. To verify the safety of its beef, the company sought permission from the USDA to incorporate the agency's "rapid test" method into its production and marketing efforts.

The testing decision proved to be controversial. The USDA opposed testing, refusing to grant Creekstone Farms permission to use the test, claiming authority under the Virus-Serum-Toxin Act (VISTA) (Robertson, 2007). The USDA claimed that the test was only to be used for "surveillance" purposes and, in the view of the USDA, "the test as proposed by Creekstone would have implied a consumer safety aspect that is not scientifically warranted" (Viña, 2006) Trade associations representing the cattle industry also opposed Creekstone Farms' efforts to test the beef (Weintraub, 2004). The rationale offered

[7] Earlier estimates of the cost of the test were $7 to $25 per head. APHIS estimated costs of $25 to $50 per animal, but these costs included other cost components, such as outreach and record-keeping costs (Lister and Becker, 2007).

by the National Cattlemen's Beef Association is that testing would mislead consumers into thinking untested beef was not safe (McNeil, Jr., 2004). Others have suggested that cost was the industry's main concern (Schlosser, 2004).

Creekstone subsequently filed a lawsuit against the USDA on March 23, 2006 in the District Court of the District of Columbia to obtain permission to use the USDA-approved BSE rapid test kits. The focus on the USDA test kit rather than other possible test kits arose because none of the five rapid tests used in Europe for cattle have been approved by the USDA for use in the U.S. (Normile, 2004). The only rapid test option was to use the USDA-authorized rapid test kit manufactured by Bio-Rad. An official at the California company Bio-Rad that developed the test said the USDA "made it very clear that they were not accepting any applications" for approval of other tests (Normile, 2004, p. 157).

Before considering the specifics of the case, it is useful to examine the underlying economics. Any such safety testing is typically subject to two classes of errors.[8] With a Type I error, the beef is safe, but the rapid test indicates that it is not. While APHIS has expressed concern regarding false positive test results, these false positives do not appear to be common, as the USDA has documented only two "inconclusive" test results (Viña, 2006). Based on some estimates, the Bio-Rad screening test has a false positive rate of 1/1,000 (Lister and Becker, 2007). If there were an error of this type, presumably it could be resolved by not marketing the beef and instead undertaking more extensive tests. Doing so would avoid the risk of creating undue alarm by suggesting that the U.S. had another BSE-infected animal when in fact there was no risk. Perhaps because this type of error could be readily addressed, it did not play a prominent role in the litigation, though the potential for false positives was used as a defense argument.

Type II errors for the rapid test would involve the certification of the beef as being free from BSE when in fact it is not. How much of a risk this error creates depends on the accuracy of the test. But, even assuming an imperfect test, the failure to find evidence of BSE does provide information in that it indicates that there is a lower probability

[8] For discussion of Type I and Type II errors generally, see Viscusi et al. (2000).

of BSE than would be the case in the absence of the test. The amount of information conveyed by the test consequently hinges on the frequency of BSE in the cattle population and the ability of the test to identify which cattle are infected and which are not. If the accuracy of the test is disclosed to officials from countries such as Japan, these sophisticated consumers of information should be able to process the informational content of the testing method being used and decide whether it is a sufficient indicator of the relative safety of the product to merit a lifting of the import ban. Japanese consumer demand seems to be promoting such action if or when beef is deemed "safe."[9]

How great a problem are Type I and Type II errors for BSE tests? The risk of false positives and undue alarm from such results does not appear great because it doesn't seem to be a major concern with government sanctioned use of the rapid test. Moreover, if there is a positive test, additional testing could be undertaken. Such subsequent testing was undertaken in the case of what turned out to be a false negative test result. In 2005, the U.S. Department of Agriculture disclosed that an animal that had tested negative for BSE in 2004 was found to be positive (McNeil, Jr. and Barrionuevo, 2005). Even though the negative test result was based on the test procedure that the USDA regarded as the "gold standard," subsequent testing of a specimen from the same animal by the pre-eminent laboratory in England found a positive test result. Thus, the gold standard rapid test can be followed by more extensive testing when there are positive test results. In practice, one would not expect negative test results that actually are false negatives to be followed by additional tests.

How such testing will play out in the market context is an example of the role of quality certification within the context of lemons markets (Viscusi, 1978). For purposes of the discussion below, we assume that consumers perceive that beef with a favorable rapid test result has a lower probability of being infected by BSE than animals that are not tested. In the standard "lemons" model, consumers assess the quality of used cars based on the average quality of used cars of that type on

[9] "Japanese importers who began purchasing beef immediately after the ban was lifted in July [2006] were unable to obtain enough, and importers who waited to judge consumer acceptance found themselves struggling to fill supply chains" (Clemens, 2007).

the market. Carrying this over to the BSE beef context, based on this formulation consumers will assess the beef as having the average risk of cattle in the U.S. of that type. Given the low incidence of BSE, unless there is a major increase in incidence rates, one would expect any such risk assessment to be extremely low and very close to zero.

What effect would there be if a producer could reliably certify its beef as safe? Firms that will reap the highest increase in profits net of testing costs will be the first to seek quality certification. Typically, one would expect companies that produce very low-risk beef to be among the first to seek such quality certification. In addition, among the first companies undertaking testing are those companies which sell beef in markets that are very intolerant of even very low risks or which require full testing for their domestic regulatory purposes. Creekstone Farms is one such company because it wanted to sell expensive and presumably more profitable cuts of beef to the Japanese market. Product image, and not simply safety, may be a concern as well.[10]

The USDA's argument that testing only high risk cattle was "the most efficient method for detecting the presence of BSE" (Robertson, 2007, p. 10) may well be correct. The USDA may have been correct that the tests were "worthless. . . when used, as proposed by plaintiff, to diagnose the disease in all slaughter-aged normal-looking cattle" (Robertson, 2007, p. 16). But being a "worthless" test because the low BSE risks means the tests have little value is quite a different matter than being worthless because the tests themselves are flawed. Competitive pressures will generally eliminate expenditures that are truly worthless to the firm. As Judge Robertson (2007) observed, it is inconsistent for the USDA to argue that the tests are "worthless" while at the same time claiming that the tests provide valuable information to the agency about the prevalence of BSE. The government generally does not have a practice of preventing companies from making wasteful resource allocation decisions. In a decentralized economy, the companies themselves are best able to judge whether the expected increase in

[10] Bailey et al. (2005) note that "[t]he private sector may also have non-price incentives for establishing farm-to-fork traceability or expanded testing such as developing or maintaining brand image or equity, identifying production efficiencies, and/or limiting product liability" (p. 4).

profits net of the testing costs will be positive. Creekstone apparently had made the judgment that testing was a sound business decision[11] and, if the decision proved to be unsound, the company would soon be able to observe its mistake. To the extent that there is any efficiency rationale for the USDA's position, it must be in terms of the efficiency ramifications that a Creekstone testing decision will have on other firms in the industry.

Suppose that Creekstone Farms is able to test and certify its beef as being safe. What will be the effect on the rest of the market? Based on the well known economics "lemons" model (Akerlof, 1970), consumers judge product groups by their average risk.[12] The fact that Creekstone Farms has in effect broken out of the market through testing will not imply that the remaining companies' beef is unsafe. Rather, the pertinent risk measure is the average risk of the beef across all the beef being sold by the remaining producers. Unless consumers believed that Creekstone Farms was a particularly low-risk producer, there should be little if any effect on the perceived risk for the remaining producers. If, however, there is an increase in the perceived risk, that in turn may lead other producers who can gain from quality certification to invest in testing. Breaking this firm away from the untested beef in the market will subsequently affect consumers' risk beliefs for the remaining uncertified beef producers, potentially leading to further unraveling in the market as more producers seek to certify their beef as being safe. Usually, one would expect unraveling to occur from the top down with the lowest risk producers seeking certification first.

Whether there will be such subsequent unraveling depends on several factors. The higher the testing costs, the less will be the willingness of firms to incur these costs to distinguish their product from the market. If the risks are very low and differ little by producer, the incentive to have the beef certified will be modest. In the absence of specialty products that cater to a market in which testing certification plays a much more important role than it would for the domestic

[11] Creekstone claimed that continuing fears of BSE harmed its profits because of its substantial export business. It also claimed that consumers would pay a higher price for tested beef (Robertson, 2007).

[12] See Viscusi (1978) for the role of quality certification in the context of this class of models.

market in which the perceived risk is the average risk of the untested beef, one would expect there to be little demand for rapid testing of cattle. There would not be complete unraveling of the market, but testing costs would be limited.

Whether any testing is efficient at all depends on the structure of the economic problem. If all beef will be eaten in the U.S., whether tested or not, the main effect of testing may be to raise the price of favorably tested beef and lower the price of the untested beef to the extent that its average risk has increased by the certification of the safety of the tested beef. In that extreme context, all testing costs are efficiency losses as testing simply serves to transfer profits to the producers that undertake testing. If, however, the testing enables consumers to better match their beef consumption to their risk preferences, which are heterogeneous across the population, then testing may serve a constructive role. More important in this instance is that we do not live in a fully efficient world. If other countries such as Japan impose bans on the importation of untested beef but will permit imports of favorably tested beef, which is behavior that from the U.S. perspective may not appear to be economically rational, then it may nevertheless be desirable to undertake testing, recognizing that U.S. producers do not operate within the context of a fully efficient world. Subject to the structure of the foreign and domestic demand for beef produced in the U.S., how should the testing issue be addressed?

While the litigation over the testing did not address all of these issues, many of these concerns played a key role in the District Court's decision to overrule the USDA prohibition on voluntary use of the USDA-approved rapid test for marketing purposes. The District Court recognized that there had been a 75 percent decline in U.S. beef exports because countries such as Japan and South Korea banned the importation of U.S. beef after the 2003 BSE incident. In response to this BSE case, APHIS introduced an enhanced surveillance program that tested cattle that APHIS designated as being of "high risk," such as cattle older than 30 months and cattle that were unable to walk (Robertson, 2007). The 26-month enhanced surveillance program identified two additional BSE cases after testing about 750,000 cattle. There continues to be government sanctioned testing of 40,000 cattle per year, but private companies such as Creekstone Farms are not permitted to test.

This limitation on private testing combines with the usage of a more comprehensive testing approach in other countries to put U.S. exports at a competitive disadvantage if importing countries have testing requirements for imported beef. As the District Court observed: "Other countries, where BSE has been found, test all or a significant portion of the cattle presented for normal slaughter. The European Union, for example, requires BSE testing not only for 'at risk' or 'suspect' cattle, but also for all apparently healthy cattle presented for slaughter for human consumption that are over 30 months of age. France, Italy, and Spain require testing of all cattle slaughtered at 24 months of age or over" (Robertson, 2007, footnote 1). The World Organisation for Animal Health (OIE) has also recommended that "deboned skeletal muscle meat [excluding mechanically separated meat] from cattle 30 months of age or less..." should not require any BSE-related conditions (e.g., tests) for trade (World Organisation for Animal Health, 2005).[13] This latter foreign testing is not, however, efficient (from a benefit-cost standpoint) or efficacious (from a safety standpoint). Because the incubation period for BSE is from two to eight years, testing cattle younger than 30 months seldom would detect a positive case of BSE. Because most U.S. cattle go to market at less than 24 months, the USDA maintains that there is no food safety value for testing.

Nevertheless, Creekstone Farms wanted to undertake the test because it was suffering lost profits and a 35 percent drop in revenues. The company estimated that it was losing $200,000 per day in revenues due to the import bans by South Korea and Japan alone. In the company's view, the partial lifting of the bans in 2006 did not eliminate the losses because of continued fears regarding its product. The company established a testing laboratory for rapid tests that would use the test procedures by Bio-Rad, Inc., which is the same testing company

[13] The most recent edition of the *Terrestrial Animal Health Code* maintains the same guidance, except that it drops the "30 months of age or less" condition (World Organisation for Animal Health, 2013a).

that produces the officially sanctioned test for the USDA. The USDA prohibited Bio-Rad from selling the test kits to Creekstone.

While the District Court did find that the USDA had substantial authority to regulate the testing, it ruled in favor of the plaintiff. The USDA had simultaneously argued that the tests were "worthless" and could be "used for treatment" of animal disease. That the tests might have a productive role in treatment and management of the BSE disease by identifying the infected cattle and their prevalence was not controversial. The District Court rejected the claim, however, that the tests were "worthless" because if cattle were infected, the disease could be detected with the test.[14]

This case illustrates the tension between the quest for economic efficiency of policies and the private self-interest that companies may have in testing. Although the USDA did not prepare a formal analysis of the *costs* and risk reduction that would result from private testing, the department's general characterization of the situation was not contradicted by the plaintiffs.

The expected number of BSE cases that would be identified by Creekstone Farms testing will be very close to zero and would not warrant the cost from the standpoint of the U.S. market if people perceive the risk accurately. What is efficient policy for the U.S., however, may not necessarily be optimal from the standpoint of exports because the refusal to allow private testing prohibits companies from undertaking the kind of testing that is the norm in countries such as Japan. Other countries' regulatory regimes, however ill conceived, do define the market in which these firms operate. Thus, the plus side

[14] The District Court concluded its ruling with this guidance for policy on testing: "In any event, evaluation of "worthlessness" (*vel non!*) is best left to the apostles of law and economics, who might find a formula for deciding whether USDA is right, that BSE testing of seemingly healthy cattle at normal slaughter age has neither scientific value nor any value to consumers, because it is likely to produce false negative results that could mislead the public — or Creekstone is right, that USDA's decision to conduct less extensive testing than other countries has left U.S. companies at a competitive disadvantage, and thus that private testing could be valuable to a seller of cattle — or I am right, that the consumer issues at the heart of USDA's position cannot be located within the purposes of the VSTA, and appear to lie, not with USDA, but with the Federal Trade Commission, or perhaps the Commerce Department" (Robertson, 2007, p. 17).

of private testing is that it would expand the export market for U.S. beef, leading to greater profits for the companies and efficiency gains from the standpoint of the U.S.

After the District Court ruled in favor of Creekstone Farms, Consumers Union urged the USDA not to appeal the decision (Hansen, 2007). In addition to opposing this intrusion on "free and open scientific inquiry" and on "free markets," Consumers Union claimed that the tests of apparently healthy cattle in Europe have identified 1,100 cases of BSE from 2001 to 2006. Moreover, its 2004 survey found that "71% of the public supported testing of cattle for BSE and, of those, some 95% were willing to spend 10 cents more per pound of meat to buy tested meat" (Hansen, 2007).

However, the USDA did appeal the decision of the District Court. In 2008 the U.S. Court of Appeals for the District of Columbia Circuit reversed the lower court's ruling that USDA did not have the authority to regulate BSE test kits, effectively banning Creekstone Farms from private testing.[15]

While permitting Creekstone Farms to test beef for export would have been a form of quality certification for foreign markets, for U.S. consumers to be able to distinguish tested beef from untested beef there needs to be some way to identify tested beef, such as through product labeling.[16] Because the Creekstone case pertained to certification for exports rather than labeling for U.S. consumption, the merits of such risk communication efforts for the U.S. market were not examined. However, the transmission of information through a labeling system for the U.S. public is a quite different matter than certifying that beef exports are in compliance with a well understood regulatory regime in another country.

How would consumers interpret the "tested for BSE" label?[17] If the meat is not labeled as having been tested, does this mean that there is no reason to believe the meat is safe? Because there is a surveillance

---

[15] *Creekstone Farms Premium Beef, L.L.C. v. U.S. Dept. of Agriculture et al.*, 539 F.3d 492, 503 (D.C. Cir. 2008).

[16] Consumers Union supports such "tested for BSE" labels (Hansen, 2007).

[17] Two studies employed surveys of Canadian households and found that a segment of consumers would be willing to pay more for beef labeled as tested for BSE (Steiner and Yang, 2010; Cranfield, 2011).

program and a series of other regulatory safeguards in place, the USDA has established a regime that does ensure a low level of risk. The task for any risk communication effort is to simultaneously convey both the low baseline risk of meat as well as any additional small reduction in risk or anxiety with respect to the risk that may be affected by testing.

10

Regulatory Policy Lessons

Based on our assessment of the mad cow experience, we have derived ten principal lessons for U.S. risk regulation.

Lesson 1. Learn from risk experiences in other countries. Because BSE and vCJD risks were apparent in the U.K. before in the U.S., there was an opportunity to use this information in formulating the feed ban policy and other regulatory responses to avert similar problems in the U.S. Because no crisis developed in the U.S., it is not clear whether regulators also profited by observing the adverse effects that conflicting scientific information and sometimes inept policy responses had on the public and on the government's credibility.

Lesson 2. Trust is an essential component of effective risk communication. For risk information to have an effect on the public's risk beliefs, the source has to have credibility. If the government jeopardizes this trust through conflicting risk information or information that seems to be tainted by economic interests, then it will lose credibility. Maintaining credibility is especially difficult when the underlying science is uncertain and changing over time. How the government should convey risk information when the risk is not well known and may change in the future merits future research as it will play a central role in future policy responses.

Lesson 3. There will be an alarmist response to new or conflicting risk information. If the experts from different groups disagree, people will believe the risk is much greater than the average of the risk estimates. In addition, newly discovered hazards in products formerly believed to be safe will tend to produce an alarmist response. Attempts to dampen these effects by asserting that the product is safe when it is not will simply undermine the government's future credibility. If the public is going to overreact to risk information, how people process risk information and whether people will behave irrationally after being given the information must be incorporated in the development of the appropriate risk communication policy.

Lesson 4. The policy objective should be to maximize the difference between expected benefits and expected costs. While this maxim may appear to be straightforward, it has important implications for risk assessment. In particular, the risk probabilities should be mean risk values rather than "conservative" worst case assumptions. Upper bound risk values not only distort policy making but also cause undue alarm, as did the worst case U.K. vCJD estimates that were based on unrealistic incubation period assumptions.

Lesson 5. Regulatory policy analyses should assess the present value of the expected benefits and costs. The initial wave of U.S. policy responses involved no benefit assessments at all, only an assessment of the costs. To the extent that benefits were discussed, they were treated in highly impressionistic terms. More recently, there has been at least one instance in which an attempt was made to assess risks, but there has been no attempt to monetize the value of expected lives saved or to estimate the benefits in consumer welfare. These are essential missing links. Given that the most cost-beneficial policies probably have already been enacted, it is essential that future regulations be subjected to full blown assessment of costs and benefits.

Lesson 6. Regulatory responses to risks should carefully discern between immediate public responses via surveys and the public's attitudes as revealed by their behavior. Several telephone surveys revealed grossly exaggerated, alarmist concerns about contracting vCJD soon after the identification of the first BSE-infected cow in the U.S. and claims that they would reduce their beef consumption. Investigations of the empirical evidence show both a very low risk of contracting vCJD through the U.S. beef supply and a short-term, modest decline in beef consumption after December 2003.

Lesson 7. Risk management policies should adjust to new risk information over time. The USDA launched a BSE surveillance program in 1990 and ramped it up significantly after detection of the first BSE-infected cow in 2003. After two years of this enhanced surveillance program yielded sufficient information on the low prevalence of BSE in the cattle population, the USDA ramped down the surveillance to a much lower rate of testing. This adjustment can free up resources to target other invasive species risks.

Lesson 8. The management of invasive species risks should equate the marginal value of risk reduction across all means of mitigating the risks. The USDA does not undertake complete benefit-cost analyses of individual rules addressing BSE, which precludes a formal assessment of the relative returns of policies on surveillance, border inspection, rendering practices, the protein content of animal feed, etc. Some policy approaches may deliver much greater net benefits than others and would justify a reallocation of resources and effort.

Lesson 9. Testing of BSE for beef exports is a legitimate form of quality certification. While the USDA opposes such testing as being inefficient, U.S. producers are acting in an imperfect world in which testing for BSE safety is part of other countries' regulatory regimes. What is efficient for the U.S. market is not acceptable for exports. Based on standard economic analyses, such testing will not taint consumer perceptions of U.S. beef given the very low level of risk that untested beef poses.

Lesson 10. Labeling of BSE tested beef for sale in the U.S. raises important risk communication issues. Suppose that some beef sold in the U.S. is labeled as having been tested for BSE and free of BSE, which would be a measure valued by a segment of the consumer public. The decision to permit explicit labeling does have informational content for unlabeled beef that merits further exploration. There might need to be an informational effort to convey to consumers what risk the untested beef had. Do consumers, for example, believe that no government regulations sought to ensure the safety of unlabelled beef? BSE test labeling may be a viable option, but before launching such an effort there must be an assessment of the most responsible way to design such a risk communication effort.

Appendix

Table A.1. Relative infectivity of specific tissues specified from an infected bovine[a].

Tissue	Fraction of total infectivity
Brain	No infectivity in cattle <32 months post-inoculation (PI) 32 months PI and over: 64.1 percent
Trigeminal Ganglia	No infectivity in cattle <32 months post-inoculation 32 months PI and over: 2.6 percent
Other Head (eyes, etc.)	No infectivity in cattle <32 months post-inoculation 32 months PI and over: 0.04 percent
Distal Ileum	6–18 months post-inoculation: 100 percent 18–31: No infectivity 32 months PI and over 3.3 percent
Spinal Cord	No infectivity in cattle <32 months post-inoculation 32 months PI and over: 25.6 percent
Dorsal Root Ganglia	No infectivity in cattle <32 months post-inoculation 32 months PI and over: 3.8 percent

[a]The post-inoculation (PI) time values in this table reflect the assumption that the incubation period is 36 months.
Source: Cohen et al. (2001), Table 3-1.

Table A.2. Number of cases of bovine spongiform encephalopathy (BSE) reported in U.K.

1987 and before	446
1988	2,514
1989	7,228
1990	14,407
1991	25,359
1992	37,280
1993	35,090
1994	24,438
1995	14,562
1996	8,149
1997	4,393
1998	3,235
1999	2,301
2000	1,443
2001	1,202
2002	1,144
2003	611
2004	343
2005	225
2006	114
2007	67
2008	37
2009	12
2010	11
2011	7
2012	3

Source: World Organisation for Animal Health, Number of Cases of Bovine Spongiform Encephalopathy (BSE) Reported in the United Kingdom, available at http://www.oie.int/en/animal-health-in-the-world/bse-specific-data/number-of-cases-in-the-united-kingdom/, (last visited February 3, 2013).

Table A.3. Number of reported cases of bovine spongiform encephalopathy (BSE) in farmed cattle worldwide.

Year	France	Germany	Ireland	Portugal	Switzerland	USA
1989	0	0	15	0	0	0
1990	0	0	14	1	2	0
1991	5	0	17	1	8	0
1992	0	1	18	1	15	0
1993	1	0	16	3	29	0
1994	4	3	19	12	64	0
1995	3	0	16	15	68	0
1996	12	0	73	31	45	0
1997	6	2	80	30	38	0
1998	18	0	83	127	14	0
1999	31	0	91	159	50	0
2000	16	7	149	149	33	0
2001	274	125	246	110	42	0
2002	239	106	333	86	24	0
2003	137	54	183	133	21	0[a]
2004	54	65	126	92	3	0
2005	31	32	69	46	3	1
2006	8	16	41	33	5	1
2007	9	4	25	14	0	0
2008	8	2	23	18	0	0
2009	10	2	9	8	0	0
2010	5	0	2	6	0	0
2011	3	0	3	5	2	0
2012	1	0	3	–	1	1

[a]One case diagnosed in December 2003 in the United States was confirmed as having been imported from Canada, and the OIE attributes this reported case to Canada.

Source: World Organisation for Animal Health, Number of Reported Cases of Bovine Spongiform Encephalopathy (BSE) in Farmed Cattle Worldwide (Excluding the United Kingdom), available at http://www.oie.int/animal-health-in-the-world/bse-specific-data/number-of-reported-cases-worldwide-excluding-the-united-kingdom/, (last visited February 3, 2013).

References

Adda, J. (2007), 'Behavior toward health risks: An empirical study using the 'mad cow' crisis as an experiment'. *Journal of Risk and Uncertainty* **35**(3), 285–305.

Akerlof, G. A. (1970), 'The market for 'lemons': Qualitative uncertainty and the market mechanism'. *The Quarterly Journal of Economic Review* **84**(3), 488–500.

Aldy, J. E. and W. K. Viscusi (2013), 'Environmental risk and uncertainty'. In: M. Machina and W. K. Viscusi (eds.): *Handbook of the Economics of Risk and Uncertainty,* vol. 1. Amsterdam: Elsevier.

Antle, J. M. (2001), 'Economic analysis of food safety'. In: B. Gardner and G. Rausser (eds.): *Handbook of Agricultural Economics,* vol. 1. Amsterdam: Elsevier.

Bailey, D., J. Robb, and L. Checketts (2005), 'Perspectives on traceability and BSE testing in the U.S. beef industry'. *Choices Magazine* **20**(4), 293–297.

Balter, M. (2000), 'Tracking the human fallout from mad cow disease'. *Science* **289**(5484), 1452–1454.

Bellaby, P. (2003), 'Communication and miscommunication of risk: Understanding U.K. parents' attitudes to combined MMR vaccination'. *British Medical Journal* **327**(7417), 725–728.

Boame, A., W. Parsons, and M. Trent (2004), 'Mad cow disease and beef trade: An update'. Statistics Canada. http://www.statcan.gc.ca/pub/11-621-m/11-621-m2004010-eng.pdf (last accessed Nov. 13, 2013).

Böelle, P.-Y., G. Thomas, A.-J. Valleron, J.-Y. Cesbron, and R. Will (2003), 'Modelling the epidemic of variant Creutzfeldt-Jakob disease in the UK based on age characteristics: Updated, detailed analysis'. *Statistical Methods in Medical Research* **12**(3), 221–233.

Boyle, J. P. (2008). President and CEO of the American Meat Institute, Testimony, Hallmark/Westland Meat Recall, Hearing Before a Subcommittee of the Committee on Appropriations, United States Senate, Feb. 28, p. 48, available at http://www.gpo.gov/fdsys/pkg/CHRG-110shrg44333/pdf/CHRG-110shrg44333.pdf (last accessed Nov. 13, 2013).

Brown, P., R. G. Will, R. Bradley, D. M. Asher, and L. Detwiler (2001), 'Bovine spongiform encephalopathy and variant Creutzfeldt-Jakob disease: Background, evolution, and current concerns'. *Emerging Infectious Diseases* **7**(1), 6–16.

Burton, M. and T. Young (1996), 'The impact of BSE on the demand for beef and other meats in Great Britain'. *Applied Economics* **28**(6), 687–693.

Burton, M. and T. Young (1997), 'Measuring meat consumers' response to the perceived risks of BSE in Great Britain'. *Risk Decision and Policy* **2**(1), 19–28.

Center for Infectious Disease Research and Policy (2004), 'Florida woman dies of probable vCJD'. University of Minnesota, June 22, available at http://www.cidrap.umn.edu/cidrap/content/other/bse/news/june2204vcjd.html (last visited Nov. 13, 2013).

Center for Infectious Disease Research and Policy (2005), 'Briton has second vCJD case found in U.S'. University of Minnesota, Nov. 22, available at http://www.cidrap.umn.edu/cidrap/content/other/bse/news/nov2205vcjd.html (last visited Nov. 13, 2013).

Center for Veterinary Medicine (1996), 'Finding of no significant impact for 21 CFR 589.2000: Prohibition of protein derived from ruminant and mink tissues in ruminant feeds'. Food and Drug Administration, Nov. 1996.

Cherfas, J. (1990), 'Mad cow disease: Uncertainty rules'. *Science* **249**(4976), 1492–1493.

Chung, C., T. Boyer, and S. Han (2009), 'Valuing quality attributes and country of origin in the Korean beef market'. *Journal of Agricultural Economics* **60**(3), 682–698.

Cleemput, I., M. Leys, D. Ramaekers, and L. Bonneux (2006), 'Balancing evidence and public opinion in health technology assessments: The case of leukoreduction'. *International Journal of Technology Assessment in Health Care* **22**(4), 403–407.

Clemens, R. (2007), 'After the ban: U.S. beef exports to Japan lag demand'. *Iowa Agricultural Review* **13**(1). available at http://www.card.iastate.edu/iowa_ag_review/winter_07/article5.aspx (last visited Nov. 13, 2013).

CNN (2008), 'USDA orders recall of 143 million pounds of beef'. Feb. 18, available at http://www.cnn.com/2008/HEALTH/02/17/beef.recall/ (last visited Nov. 13, 2013).

Coffey, B., J. Mintert, S. Fox, T. Schroeder, and L. Valentin (2005a), 'The economic impact of BSE: A research summary'. Kansas State University Agricultural Experiment Station and Cooperative Extension Service, MF-2679, May 2005.

Coffey, B., J. Mintert, S. Fox, T. Schroeder, and L. Valentin (2005b), 'The economic impact of BSE on the U.S. beef industry: Product value losses, regulatory costs, and consumer reactions'. Kansas State University Agricultural Experiment Station and Cooperative Extension Service, MF-2678, April 2005.

Cohen, J. T. and G. M. Gray (2003), 'Evaluation of the Potential Spread of BSE in Cattle and Possible Human Exposure Following Introduction of Infectivity into the United States from Canada'. Harvard Center for Risk Analysis, Harvard School of Public Health.

Cohen J. et al. (2001), 'Evaluation of the potential for bovine spongiform encephalopathy in the United States'. Report to the U.S. Department of Agriculture, Harvard Center for Risk Analysis, Harvard School of Public Health, available at http://www.foodsafety.k-state.edu/articles/332/bse_eval_US.pdf (last accessed Nov. 13, 2013).

Cousens, S. N., E. Vynnycky, M. Zeidler, R. G. Will, and P. G. Smith (1997), 'Predicting the CJD epidemic in humans'. *Nature* **385**, 197–198.

Cranfield, J. (2011), 'Consumer acceptance and valuation of beef that has been tested for BSE'. Selected paper prepared for the Agricultural & Applied Economics Association 2011 AAEA/NAREA Joint Annual Meeting, Pittsburgh, Pennsylvania July 24-26, 2011.

Creekstone Farms Premium Beef, L.L.C. v. U.S. Dept. of Agriculture et al., 517 F Supp.2d 8 (D.D.C. Mar. 29, 2007).

Creekstone Farms Premium Beef, L.L.C. v. U.S. Dept. of Agriculture et al., 539 F.3d 492, 503 (D.C. Cir. 2008).

Curnow, R. N. (1999), 'Unfathomable nature and government policy'. *The Statistician* **48**(4), 463–476.

Dickinson, D. L. and D. Bailey (2005), 'Experimental evidence on willingness-to-pay for red meat traceability in the United States, Canada, the United Kingdom, and Japan'. *Journal of Agriculture and Applied Economics* **37**(3), 537–548.

Ding, Y., M. M. Veeman, and W. L. Adamowicz (2011), 'Habit, BSE, and the dynamics of feed consumption'. *Canadian Journal of Agricultural Economics* **59**(3), 337–359.

Eastern Research Group (1997), 'Cost analysis of regulatory options to reduce the risk of an outbreak of transmissible spongiform encephalopathies (TSEs) in the United States'. Addendum to Final Report to the FDA, April 30, 1997.

Eastern Research Group (1999), 'Cost analysis of regulatory options to reduce the risk of an outbreak of transmissible spongiform encephalopathies (TSEs) in the United States'. Final Report to the FDA, Dec. 31, 1999.

Eastern Research Group (2005a), 'Economic impacts of alternative changes to the FDA regulation of animal feeds to address the risk of bovine spongiform encephalopathies'. Final Report to the FDA, July 25, 2005.

Eastern Research Group (2005b), 'Economic impacts of proposed FDA regulatory changes of animal feeds due to risk of bovine spongiform encephalopathies'. Final Report to the FDA, July 25, 2005.

Ellsberg, D. (1961), 'Risk, ambiguity, and the savage axioms'. *Quarterly Journal of Economics* **75**(4), 643–669.

Food Safety and Inspection Service (2004), 'Prohibition of the use of specified risk materials for human food and requirements for the disposition of non-ambulatory disable cattle'. *Federal Register* **69**(7), 1861–1874.

Food Safety and Inspection Service (2005), 'Preliminary analysis of interim final rules and an interpretive rule to prevent the BSE agent from entering the U.S. food supply'.

Fox, C. R. and A. Tversky (1995), 'Ambiguity aversion and comparative ignorance'. *Quarterly Journal of Economics* **110**(3), 585–603.

Fox, J., B. Coffey, J. Mintert, T. Schroeder, and L. Valentin (2005), 'The response to BSE in the United States'. *Choices Magazine* **20**(2), 103–107.

Fox, J. A. and H. H. Peterson (2004), 'Risks and implications of bovine spongiform encephalopathy for the United States: Insights from other countries'. *Food Policy* **29**(1), 45–60.

Gayer, T., J. T. Hamilton, and W. K. Viscusi (2000), 'Private values of risk tradeoffs at Superfund sites: Housing market evidence on learning about risk'. *Review of Economics and Statistics* **32**(3), 439–451.

Ghani, A. C., N. M. Ferguson, C. A. Donnelly, and R. M. Anderson (2003), 'Short-term projections for variant Creutzfeldt-Jakob disease onsets'. *Statistical Methods in Medical Research* **12**(3), 191–201.

Gray, G., M. D. Rogers, and J. B. Wiener (2011), 'Beef, hormones, and mad cows'. In: J. B. Wiener, M. D. Rogers, J. K. Hammitt, and P. H. Sand (eds.): *The Reality of Precaution: Comparing Risk Regulation in the United States and Europe*. Washington, DC: RFF Press.

Hamilton, J. T. and W. K. Viscusi (1999), *Calculating Risks? The Spatial and Political Dimensions of Hazardous Waste Policy*. Cambridge: MIT Press.

Hansen, M. (2007), 'Court ruled Creekstone Farms allowed to use rapid test kits to screen their cattle for BSE'. Letter from Michael Hansen, Senior Scientist, Consumers Union, to Honorable Michael Johanns, Secretary of Agriculture, available at http://consumersunion.org/news/court-ruled-creekstone-farms-allowed-to-use-rapid-test-kits-to-screen-their-cattle-for-bse/ (last visited Nov. 13, 2013).

Harvard Center for Risk Analysis and Center for Computational Epidemiology (2002). Review of the Evaluation of the Potential for Bovine Spongiform Encephalopathy in the United States Conducted by the Harvard Center for Risk Analysis, Harvard School of Public Health and Center for Computational Epidemiology, College of Veterinary Medicine, Tuskegee University, RTI Project Number 07182.024.

Hassouneh, I., T. Serra, and J. M. Gil (2010), 'Price transmission in the Spanish bovine sector: The BSE effect'. *Agricultural Economics* **41**(1), 33–42.

Huillard d'Aignaux, J. N., S. N. Cousens, and P. G. Smith (2001), 'Predictability of U.K. variant Creutzfeldt-Jakob disease epidemic'. *Science* **294**(5547), 1729–1731.

Huillard d'Aignaux, J. N., S. N. Cousens, and P. G. Smith (2003), 'The predictability of the epidemic of variant Creutzfeldt-Jakob disease by back-calculation methods'. *Statistical Methods in Medical Research* **12**(3), 203–220.

Ishida, T., N. Ishikawa, and M. Fukushige (2010), 'Impact of BSE and bird flu on consumers' meat demand in Japan'. *Applied Economics* **42**(1), 49–56.

Jin, H. J. and W. W. Koo (2003), 'The effect of the BSE outbreak in Japan on consumers' preferences'. *European Review of Agricultural Economics* **30**(2), 173–192.

Jin, Y. H., G. J. Power, and L. Elbakidze (2008), 'The impact of North American BSE events on live cattle and futures prices'. *American Journal of Agricultural Economics* **90**(5), 1279–1286.

Johnecheck, W. A. (2010), 'Consumer information, marks of origin, and WTO Law: A case study of the United States — certain country of origin labeling requirements dispute'. Food Policy and Applied Nutrition Program Discussion Paper No. 43, Friedman School of Nutrition Science and Policy.

Jones, B. (2008), 'Md. schools touched by beef recall'. *Baltimore Sun,* Feb. 20.

Jones, K. G., A. Somwaru, and J. B. Whitaker (2009), 'Country of origin labeling: Evaluating the impacts on U.S. and world markets'. *Agricultural and Resource Economics Review* **38**(3), 397–405.

Kim, V. and J. Wilson (2008), 'Meat is a mystery to schools'. *Los Angeles Times,* Feb. 22.

Kuchler, F. and A. Tegene (2006), 'Did BSE announcements reduce beef purchases?'. Economic Research Report No. (ERR-34).

Lanska, D. J. (1998), 'The mad cow problem in the U.K.: Risk perceptions, risk management, and health policy development'. *Journal of Public Health Policy* **19**(2), 160–183.

Lim, K. H., L. J. Maynard, W. Hu, and E. Goddard (2013), 'U.S. consumers' preference and willingness to pay for country-of-origin-labeled beef steak and food safety enhancements'. *Canadian Journal of Agricultural Economics* **61**(1), 93–118.

Lister, S. A. and G. S. Becker (2007), 'Bovine spongiform encephalopathy (BSE, or 'mad cow' disease): Current and proposed safeguards'. CRS Report for Congress.

Löfstedt, R. (2005), *Risk Management in Post-Trust Societies.* London: Palgrave Macmillan.

Marsh, J. M., G. W. Brester, and V. H. Smith (2008), 'Effects of North American BSE events on U.S. cattle prices'. *Review of Agricultural Economics* **30**(1), 136–150.

Martin, A. (2008), 'Largest recall of ground beef is ordered'. *New York Times,* Feb. 18.

Mathews, Jr., K. H., M. Vandeveer, and R. A. Gustafson (2006), 'An economic chronology of Bovine Spongiform Encephalopathy in North America'. United States Department of Agriculture, Economic Research Service, LDP-M-143-01.

McCluskey, J. J., K. M. Grimsrud, H. Ouchi, and T. I. Wahl (2005), 'Bovine spongiform encephalopathy in Japan: Consumers' food safety perceptions and willingness to pay for tested beef'. *Australian Journal of Agricultural & Resource Economics* **49**(2), 197–209.

McNeil, Jr., D. G. (2004), 'U.S. won't let company test all its cattle for mad cow'. *New York Times,* April 10.

McNeil, Jr., D. G. and A. Barrionuevo (2005), 'For months, agriculture department delayed announcing results of mad cow test'. *New York Times,* June 26.

Mutondo, J. E., B. W. Brorsen, and S. R. Henneberry (2009), 'Welfare impacts of BSE-driven trade bans'. *Agricultural and Resource Economics Review* **38**(3), 324–329.

National Creutzfeldt-Jakob Disease Research & Surveillance Unit (NCJDRSU) (2013), 'Creutzfeldt-Jakob disease in the UK (by calendar year)'. April 11, available at http://www.cjd.ed.ac.uk/documents/figs.pdf (last accessed Nov. 11, 2013).

National Safety Council (2007), *National Safety Council Injury Facts.* Itasca: National Safety Council.

Normile, D. (2004), 'First U.S. case of mad cow sharpens debate over testing'. *Science* **303**(5655), 156–157.

Pacelle, W. (2008). President and CEO of Humane Society of the United States, Testimony, Hallmark/Westland Meat Recall, Hearing Before a Subcommittee of the Committee on Appropriations, United States Senate, Feb. 28, p. 34, available at http://www.gpo.gov/fdsys/pkg/CHRG-110shrg44333/pdf/CHRG-110shrg44333.pdf (last accessed Nov. 13, 2013).

Phillips, L., J. Bridgeman, and M. Ferguson-Smith (2000), 'The BSE inquiry report'. (See Volume 6, Chapter 4, Paragraph 4.479, p. 348), available at http://collections.europarchive.org/tna/20090505194948/http://bseinquiry.gov.uk/pdf/volume6/Chapter4. pdf (last accessed Nov. 13, 2013).

Risling, G. (2008), 'USDA orders nation's largest beef recall'. *Associated Press,* Feb. 17.

Robertson, J. (2007). *Creekstone Farms Premium Beef, L.L.C. v. U.S. Dept. of Agriculture et al.*, 517 F. Supp.2d 8 (D.D.C. Mar. 29, 2007).

Sample, I. (2007), 'Should we still be worried?'. *The Guardian.* Jan. 9, available at http://www.guardian.co.uk/society/2007/jan/10/health.bse (last visited Nov. 13, 2013).

Schafer, E. T. (2008). Secretary of Agriculture, Department of Agriculture, Testimony, Hallmark/Westland Meat Recall, Hearing before a Subcommittee of the Committee on Appropriations, United States Senate, Feb. 28, p. 10, available at http://www.gpo.gov/fdsys/pkg/CHRG-110shrg44333/pdf/CHRG-110shrg44333.pdf (last visited Nov. 13, 2013).

Schlenker, W. and S. B. Villas-Boas (2009), 'Consumer and market responses to mad-cow disease'. *American Journal of Agricultural Economics* **91**(4), 1140–1152.

Schlosser, E. (2004), 'The cow jumped over the U.S.D.A.'. *New York Times,* Jan. 2.

Serra, T. (2011), 'Food scare crises and price volatility: The case of the BSE in Spain'. *Food Policy* **36**(2), 179–185.

Southeast Farm Press (2007), 'USDA proposes new BSE import rules'. Jan. 25, available at http://southeastfarmpress.com/news/012507-bse-imports (last visited Nov. 13, 2013).

Sparks Company, Inc. (2001), 'The rendering industry: Economic impact of future feedings regulations'. Report to the National Renderers Association, June.

Steiner, B. E. and J. Yang (2010), 'How do U.S. and Canadian consumers value credence attributes associated with beef labels after the North American BSE crisis of 2003?'. *International Journal of Consumer Studies* **34**(4), 449–463.

The Economist (1996), 'Mad cows and Englishmen'. Mar. 30 **406**(8829), 25.

Thomas, P. and M. Newly (1999), 'Estimating the size of the outbreak of new-variant CJD'. *British Food Journal* **101**(1), 44–58.

Tsigas, M., J. Grimalva, N. Grossman, and J. Kowalski (2008), 'Commodity trade analysis in a general equilibrium framework: BSE restrictions on beef imports from the United States and Canada'. SSRN Working Paper, Washington, D.C.: U.S. International Trade Commission.

U.S. Department of Agriculture (2008a), 'Questions and answers Hallmark/Westland Meat Packing Company'. Updated March 6, 2008, available at http://www.usda.gov/documents/usda_action_QA.pdf (last accessed Nov. 13, 2013).

U.S. Department of Agriculture (2008b), 'Transcript of technical briefing regarding Hallmark/Westland Meat Packing Company two year product recall'. Release No. 0047.08, Feb. 17.

U.S. Government Accountability Office (2002), 'Mad cow disease: Improvements in the animal feed ban and other regulatory areas would strengthen U.S. prevention efforts'. Report to Congressional Requesters, GAO-02-183.

U.S. Government Accountability Office (2005), 'Mad cow disease: FDA's management of the feed ban has improved, but oversight weaknesses continue to limit program effectiveness'. Report to Congressional Requesters, GAO-05-101.

Valleron, A.-J., P.-Y. Böelle, R. Will, and J.-Y. Cesbron (2001), 'Estimation of epidemic size and incubation time based on age characteristics of vCJD in the United Kingdom'. *Science* **294**(5547), 1726–1728.

van Zwanenberg, P. and E. Millstone (2005), *BSE: Risk, Science and Governance.* New York: Oxford University Press.

Vargas, T. (2008), 'Schools in Md., Va. set aside recalled beef'. *Washington Post,* Feb. 20.

Viña, S. R. (2006), 'The private testing of mad cow disease: Legal issues'. CRS Report for Congress, Oct. 3.

Viscusi, W. K. (1978), 'A note on 'lemons' markets with quality certification'. *Bell Journal of Economics* **9**(1), 277–279.

Viscusi, W. K. (1997), 'Alarmist decisions with divergent risk information'. *The Economic Journal* **107**(445), 1657–1670.

Viscusi, W. K. and J. E. Aldy (2003), 'The value of a statistical life: A critical review of market estimates throughout the world'. *Journal of Risk and Uncertainty* **27**(1), 5–76.

Viscusi, W. K. and H. Chesson (1999), 'Hopes and fears: The conflicting effects of risk ambiguity'. *Theory and Decision* **47**(2), 157–184.

Viscusi, W. K., J. M. Vernon, and J. E. Harrington (2000), *Economics of Regulation and Antitrust.* Cambridge: MIT Press.

Wall, P. (2007), 'Risk communication in a global environment'. Presentation at the International Symposium on Food Safety, Hong Kong, China, Jan. 12-13.

Wall Street Journal (2004), 'Fifth of Americans say mad cow in U.S. will affect eating habits'. Jan. 13.

Weintraub, A. (2004), 'Commentary: A bum steer on mad cow disease'. *Business Week,* Jan. 12.

Wieck, C. and D. W. Holland (2010), 'The economic effect of the Canadian BSE outbreak on the U.S. economy'. *Applied Economics* **42**(8), 935–946.

Wiersma, S., S. Cooper, R. Knight, A. M. Kennedy, S. Joiner, E. Belay, and L. B. Schonberger (2002), 'Probable variant Creutzfeldt-Jakob disease in a U.S. resident — Florida, 2002'. *Morbidity and Mortality Weekly Report* **51**(41), 927–929. available at http://www.cdc.gov/MMWR/preview/mmwrhtml/mm5141a3.htm (last visited Nov. 14, 2013).

Wigle, R., J. Weerahewa, M. Bredahl, and S. Samarajeewa (2007), 'Impacts of BSE on world trade in cattle and beef: Implications for the Canadian economy'. *Canadian Journal of Agricultural Economics* **55**(4), 535–549.

World Organisation for Animal Health (2005), 'Bovine spongiform encephalopathy'. In: *OIE Terrestrial Animal Health Code*. Chap. 2.3.13.

World Organisation for Animal Health (2013a), 'Bovine spongiform encephalopathy'. In: *OIE Terrestrial Animal Health Code*. Chap. 11.5.

World Organisation for Animal Health (2013b), 'Number of cases of bovine spongiform encephalopathy (BSE) reported in the United Kingdom'. Oct. 11, available at http://www.oie.int/animal-health-in-the-world/bse-specific-data/number-of-cases-in-the-united-kingdom/ (last visited Nov. 14, 2013).

World Organisation for Animal Health (2013c), 'Number of reported cases of bovine spongiform encephalopathy (BSE) in farmed cattle worldwide (excluding the United Kingdom)'. June, available at http://www.oie.int/?id= 505 (last visited Nov. 14, 2013).

Lightning Source UK Ltd.
Milton Keynes UK
UKOW05f0958230514

232173UK00001B/49/P

9 781601 987648